The Secrets
of the
Seven
Alchemists

HARRIMAN HOUSE LTD

3A Penns Road

Petersfield

Hampshire

GU32 2EW

GREAT BRITAIN

Tel: +44 (0)1730 233870

Email: enquiries@harriman-house.com

Website: www.harriman-house.com

First published in Great Britain in 2014

Copyright © Harriman House

Figures and photographs copyright © respective sources and owners.

The right of John Rosling to be identified as the Author has been asserted in accordance with the Copyright, Designs and Patents Act 1988.

ISBN: 9780857194022

British Library Cataloguing in Publication Data

A CIP catalogue record for this book can be obtained from the British Library.

Typeset by e-Digital Design Ltd.

Design by Harriman House / C.A.W.P.

The Secrets of the Seven Alchemists

A Blueprint for Business Success
Taking You to £10 Million and Beyond

John Rosling

Every owner of a physical copy of The Secrets of the Seven Alchemists *can download the eBook for free direct from us at Harriman House, in a DRM-free format that can be read on any eReader, tablet or smartphone – simply head to*

ebooks.harriman-house.com/sevenalchemists

to get your copy now.

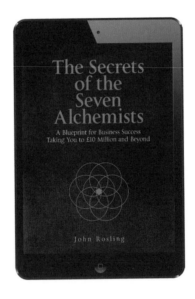

Contents

"There is more to life than increasing its speed."

Mohandas K. Gandhi

About the author

John started his career with Unilever in the UK and Japan before moving to Diageo. Since leaving the corporate world he has established and run numerous small businesses, most recently as CEO of international business performance company Shirlaws.

John speaks widely on business and entrepreneurial subjects and lectures on entrepreneurship at leading business schools. He was runner up in the 2012 Institute of Directors (IoD) Director of the Year award and is author of the popular guide for CEOs *More Money, More Time, Less Stress*.

He lives a semi-aquatic life in Hampshire with his wife and three children.

Acknowledgements

This is not my book, I have simply curated the thoughts of others. I have had the rare privilege to take down the stories of remarkable people and this is their book.

It would not have been possible without the creative genius and entrepreneurial insight of Darren Shirlaw, whose extraordinary approach to business underpins this book.

It would not exist without the words of some remarkable entrepreneurs and leaders who have given hours of their time to share their journey with humour, patience and generosity. These are both the subject of and inspiration for what follows.

Introduction

How a pig in a space helmet changed my life

I T WAS MARCH 1999, THE HEIGHT OF THE DOTCOM BOOM, AND, AS fledgling entrepreneurs, some friends and I felt somewhat left out. So we founded an e-business. And since, in common with pretty much everyone else at the time, we didn't know the first thing about the internet, we chose to create an online business in an area that we felt we could get to grips with fairly easily – greetings cards.

It was a brilliant idea but our execution was naively audacious in its complexity. Our product involved sourcing content from hundreds of separate brands and organisations, agreement to make donations to 50 charities, with a revenue model based on sponsorship from dozens of top brands. *How could it fail?*

In the same year a young commodities trader called Nick Jenkins also founded an internet greetings card business. His model was centred simply on a brilliant system. Nick built his business – Moonpig. com – to become a dominant brand with a £120m valuation (and a uniquely irritating jingle).

Our business ended up, swiftly and ignominiously, in the Receivers Court.

I have been driven ever since to understand why some ideas grow into large, valuable businesses like Moonpig.com whilst some end with a dejected huddle of ex-directors in a dreary pub opposite the Insolvency Service offices. What did Nick know that we didn't?

The answers I have found to this question in the decade since I began to think about it are contained in this book.

We are always told by business gurus that we should start a business doing something we already know. Whilst that may be good advice, it's not the whole answer. Our ignorance of the internet certainly didn't help, but Nick Jenkins was in the same boat. We were both in a whole new industry. He just tackled it differently. To quote Nick:

> "I decided that if I was going to start a business I didn't understand it might as well be something that no one else understood either."

Sector knowledge gives you a good head start but all great businesses must eventually transcend both the initial product and the experience and knowledge of the founders. What Nick instinctively knew, and we didn't, was how to see his business as *more than just a product*.

Being too focused on product or market can stifle long-term success. All truly successful businesses focus on and develop a complex inter-related set of stuff that in this book I'll call *assets*. These are the intangible drivers in your business; they're not on your balance sheet. They are the secret alchemy of your business that fuels its growth and gives it real, sustainable value. The importance of this alchemy and my thoughts on how you understand it and make it work for your business is why this book exists. Read on only if you want to create a high-value, wealth-generative business, or group of businesses, that is easy to run and a joy to own.

I think Nick's genius was in understanding this alchemy – in understanding his core assets in all their complexity. Or maybe he just got lucky.

The Seven Alchemists

The theme of this book is businesses that have reached a value of £10m or more. I will explore the journey of the entrepreneur to – and well past – that milestone. The lessons are, I hope, useful for those running private businesses of any size, but the real focus is the shift from the typical £1m to £5m business to £10m and well beyond.

In writing I have spoken to many people and at great length to seven remarkable entrepreneurs who have each built their businesses to at least a £10m valuation and in some cases many times that. There is nothing exceptional about the business sectors they are operating in and they have no inventions that have changed the world. In fact there is nothing remarkable in their stories other than the brilliance with which they have built the assets in their businesses. That is their alchemy.

This book is the story of these asset journeys. It is a distillation of the wisdom and experience of these seven business alchemists and others. It is my hope that this combined wisdom and experience will help you on your own path to building your asset-rich business, whether that is up to a value of £10m or £100m.

Why *seven* alchemists? I could explain sagely that there are seven elements in the ancient practice of alchemy. Or that in Taoism there are seven alchemy formulas to achieve the true immortal self. Or just that seven seemed a good number at the time. Take your pick.

> *"The secret of life, though, is to fall seven times and to get up eight times."*

Paulo Coelho, *The Alchemist*

(Nearly) the highest mountain in the world

The highest mountain in the world is Everest (or Chomolungma if you want to be courteous to the people who own it) at 8848 metres. The second is K2 (8611m) and the third (to win that pub quiz) is Kangchenjunga (8586m). The highest mountain outside of the Himalayan range is Aconcagua in the Andes, at just under 7000m.

Some years ago, when I was young and foolish, a good friend of mine persuaded me to climb Aconcagua. It was, without doubt, the most abjectly miserable three weeks of my adult life, during which I learnt a great deal about Siege Climbing. But it also taught me a lot about business.

Climbing a mountain is a lot like building a business: logistics; the critical importance of the team; systemisation; laying down a strategy in progressive stages and fully implementing each to build towards a clear goal; leadership; and belief. It's just that I've had more fun building a business. In fact I've had more fun at the dentist. But the mountain will give me a useful analogy to play with as we embark on this journey.

"Everyone can rise above their circumstances and achieve success if they are dedicated to and passionate about what they do."

Nelson Mandela

Introducing
the Alchemists

Keith Abel

Before I met Keith for the first time I was told that he was "charming, hilarious, self-effacing – but don't be fooled." The success story of Keith's business, Abel & Cole, is an inspiring tale of a business built by brilliant people on the basis of sound principles and obsessive focus on doing things right. The source of all of that is a charming, hilarious and self-effacing entrepreneur.

Keith will always begin his story by describing how he failed his Bar exams and started selling potatoes door-to-door in Catford, London. Potatoes developed into a range of vegetables, the famous Veg Boxes, eggs and milk. In 1991, he converted to supplying only organic vegetables, buying directly from farmers. Twenty-five years later Keith's online business turns over £65m and employs over 600 people, delivering organic food directly to over 75,000 customers.

What Abel & Cole tellingly say about themselves is:

> "We speak to our farmers every day, we know how to have a giggle, and we're still enormously grateful to our customers for keeping the whole venture alive."

www.abelandcole.co.uk

Ajaz Ahmed

Ajaz Ahmed founded AKQA when he was 21-years-old to "help organisations create the future." His company was recently valued at over half a billion dollars. Today, AKQA employs 1500 people and is the world's most awarded innovation agency. Clients include Nike, Google, Audi and Red Bull.

Ajaz co-authored *Velocity*, the number one bestselling book, alongside Nike's head of digital sport, Stefan Olander. *Velocity* has been translated into five languages and features an introduction by Sir Richard Branson. All Ajaz's proceeds from *Velocity* are donated to youth, homeless, education, global healthcare and environment causes through the Virgin Unite foundation.

@ajaz | www.AKQA.com

Frank Bastow

Frank Bastow is one of the most inspiring people I have met. Literally a perfectionist, Frank has built at least five businesses that I am aware of – all based on the core asset of making things easier.

Frank was always a star, attaining his Bronze swimming award in 1969, and going on to be the singer and bass guitarist for a cult '80s indie band (very cult, I think) and winning twice on the European Poker Tour.

Having worked within the family building and contracting company (Bastows, **www.bastows.co.uk**) for several years, in his late 20s he started Tremayne Ltd, undertaking building and decorating contracts in London. He then merged the two companies in 2000 and embarked on a huge rebranding and expansion programme. A family business since 1919, Bastows is a property restoration and redecoration company serving London's premier residential landlords and their resident tenants.

He's just published his first book, *Don't be a Can't – A Manual for Happiness*, because he wants to share some of his discoveries with the world and to try to stop us all doing stupid stuff (**www.dontbeacant.co.uk**).

Frank's other companies are Azure (**www.azurefinancialservices.com**), an accountancy firm, Hindsight (**www.hindsightsoftware.com**), a software company, and Treacle Tiger (**www.treacletiger.com**), an HR and wellbeing company.

Nick Jenkins

Nick Jenkins was a commodities trader at Glencore before he revolutionised the way we buy and send greetings cards by launching Moonpig.com in July 2000. Now it is the largest online personalised greetings card site in the world, also offering its services in Australia and the USA.

In 2011, Nick sold Moonpig.com to PhotoBox in a deal valued at £120m.

www.moonpig.com

Rupert Lee-Browne

Rupert Lee-Browne is CEO and founder of Caxton FX, the leading online currency company. He has driven Caxton's substantial year-on-year growth since it was founded in 2002 with one telephone and £25k in savings. His commitment to giving value to clients has seen the business develop into the multinational brand that it is today, with the business turnover now reaching over £600m. He is also a remarkably amusing lunch companion.

Caxton FX remains at the forefront of innovation in foreign exchange and international payments. Caxton FX became the first foreign exchange company to offer a simple online international payment system and in 2007 launched a range of prepaid currency cards. Innovation in technology is in Caxton's DNA and it continues to develop new, more efficient systems for the benefit of its customers.

Rupert's role today sees him guide the business, helping the team to progress and innovate so that Caxton FX maintains its position among the leaders in its industry. He is a keen champion of SME interests, regularly appearing in the press and at events providing his unique insight and advice for growing businesses. He currently serves as the Deputy Chair of the UK Money Transmitters Association.

www.caxtonfx.com

Roger Philby

Roger Philby is founder and CEO of The Chemistry Group, a unique – and, frankly, amazing – consulting firm delivering rapid top-line growth through behavioural change. Their focus on people and behaviour change creates amazing returns for large organisations.

What they say about themselves is:

> "Giving people opportunities to be brilliant can start with making sure your recruitment process hires those people who will thrive in your organisation, or re-energising and developing the great people you already have to be brilliant every day. Having the very best people in the very best place in your organisation is not rocket science, but it might be Chemistry."

Roger has 16 years' experience of hiring and creating best in class resourcing and development solutions in some of today's toughest talent markets and geographies. A true resourcing practitioner, he started Chemistry after finding the recruitment and talent consulting market in general bereft of any new thinking or customer-centric solutions. He thought talent management was being done so badly that the only way he could change the market was to do it better himself!

www.thechemistrygroup.com

Russell Stinson

Russell Stinson is one of the four founders and owners of ACT Clean, a business that provides essential outsourced services to London's five-star hospitality sector, employing some 1300 team members. Russell has overseen the development, processes and systems that ensure that the business runs efficiently and smoothly and gives clients assurance that everything is aligned to deliver the best possible service.

After graduating from Brunel University with a BSc Hons in Computing in Business, Russell became a software developer in the City of London. Moving to the hospitality sector, he put his business skills into action as finance director and then as managing director at Aquila Support Services.

Since forming ACT Clean in 2006, Russell and his fellow directors have worked hard to develop an ethical and values-based business that is built on strong foundations with the potential to grow as London's domination in the global five-star hospitality market continues.

www.act-clean.com

Commodore Jerry Kyd RN

Educated at Southampton University, Jerry Kyd joined the Royal Navy as a Seaman Officer in 1985 and spent his early career at sea in various ships, including aircraft carriers, frigates and the Fishery Protection Squadron. In the 1990s, he qualified as a Gunnery Officer and Specialist Navigator, and saw active service in operations in Northern Ireland, Kosovo and the Gulf.

In the last decade, in addition to instructional duties at the Maritime Warfare School as a teacher on the Specialist Navigator Course, he served as the Navigating Officer of HMS *Ark Royal* and commanded the Type 23 frigate HMS *Monmouth*.

Leaving the sea temporarily, he spent four busy years in the Ministry of Defence, where he was responsible initially for the Global Combat Ship project in the Department of Equipment Capability before selection to serve as the Military Assistant and Deputy Principal Staff Officer to the Chief of the Defence Staff.

After attending the Higher Command and Staff Course, he commanded the strike carrier HMS *Ark Royal* before moving across to HMS *Illustrious* as she worked up from her refit in the commando carrier role. Leaving 'Lusty' in early 2012, he returned to the Ministry of Defence as the Assistant Head of the Directorate of Operational Capability before taking Command of Britannia Royal Naval College in September 2012.

Commodore Jerry Kyd is married and has four sons. His other interests include keeping fit, shooting, improving his alpine skiing and, as a Yachtmaster (Offshore), sailing in home waters.

Chapter 1.
Business Alchemy

"Measuring the value of our business is about driving our strategic direction. Too many people concentrate on what they're earning but we wanted to build something that has the ability to grow and grow. We see our business as an asset."

Russell Stinson

The formula that drives business value

HERE ARE MANY CRITICAL FORMULAS IN THE WORLD. $E=mc^2$ is fairly useful if you want to build an atomic bomb. $t=\sqrt{2h/g}$ is handy when your parachute doesn't open and you want to know how long you have before you hit the ground. But if you want to know how much your business is worth now and how to build towards your vision, the formula you need to know is:

$$V = P \times M$$

That is, the value of your business (V) is a function of current profit (P) times a multiple (M).

OK, that's hardly rocket science I admit. But it is how you *use* this formula that is critical.

So, let me ask you this:

1. Can you tell me, to within a few quid, what your EBIT (or however you measure profit) was last year?

2. And now can you tell me the current and precise multiplier of that profit that determines the value of your business?

Let me guess, you've answered "Yes" to (1) and "mmmmm" to (2)? Both sides of this equation – the P and the M – are equally valid in determining the future value of your business and yet many businesses focus all of their energy on only one side.

Consider how much time you and your staff spend on increasing revenue and reducing cost. Consider how many pages of your business plan were devoted to revenue and profits. And now consider how much time you spend thinking about and creating strategies to drive the *multiple*.

Not much? That's a pity because driving the multiple can be easier and a lot more fun.

At this point those running businesses will often say, "but the market controls the multiple." They are, of course, correct. In the same way the market controls what your house is worth. But if you had two years before you were planning to sell your house, might you make some changes to increase its value? Might you upgrade the property, build an extension, put in a new bathroom? You'd presumably do more than just flick the breadmaker on a few minutes before a prospective buyer came round? In other words you would strategically invest in the *assets* of your property over time to try to increase its value.

Your business is no different. *You control* the multiple just as much as you control your profit. If you want to build a truly valuable business that will give you wealth, freedom and fulfilment, then you need to start seeing your business as a set of *defined assets* and investing in these.

At this point I have to make one thing clear: it doesn't matter if you have no intention of selling your business.

Building your business from an asset perspective is simply the best way to build a great business that is easy to run and a joy to own. It is the best way to build a business which will become increasingly independent of you, whether that independence looks like a sale or just more time for you to spend on the beach, or with the kids.

Russell Stinson, Alchemist and founder of ACT Clean, sums all of this up:

> "Measuring the value of our business is about driving our strategic direction. We want to make sure that there is something else in our business aside from products. It is important because we're not looking to do something just from a monthly financial return. We're a people business. We're building something that we want to be proud of. Too many people concentrate on what they're earning but we wanted to build something that has real foundations, that has the ability to grow and grow and not be based on any individual running it. We see our business as an asset."

It's no coincidence that Russell and his partners have built, from a standing start, a business employing 1300 people in seven years.

The seven layers of valuation

So, what are these assets and how do you use them to build a high-value business? That is of course the BIG question and why this book is over 300 pages long.

For now let's just accept that what I call assets are a set of specific, intangible things that your business contains, the combination of which defines its value. Investing in these assets and *fully implementing* appropriate strategies in a particular order is the secret to building a high-value and truly great business.

The reason these assets drive your multiple is no great mystery. It is, of course, because they determine the *future profitability* of your business, or because someone else will see value in them and look to acquire these assets to drive the future profitability of their own business. Building the things in your business today that will drive incremental, sustainable profit tomorrow increases the present-day value of the business.

However, building and strengthening these assets in your business also creates the kind of business you want to own, your customers want to buy from and your team wants to spend their time in.

At this point I want to introduce you to the seven layers of valuation. This model will be our constant companion over the coming chapters so we might as well get familiar with it now.

V+7	Scale
V+6	Brand architecture
V+5	Channel extension
V+4	Product extension
V+3	Systems / product innovation
V+2	Talent / capability / culture
V1	——————————————— Industry benchmark

This is a deceptively simple model but one that, in my experience, has the power to transform how you run your business and the wealth and freedom that you generate. What this model reveals are the specific intangible assets I referred to above and the specific order that will most effectively drive the *multiple* and therefore the value of the business.

To understand the anatomy of this framework, you need to accept the idea that there is an average multiple in any business sector. This is the average multiple of earnings achieved upon sale of a business within that sector. That is referred to in the model as the *benchmark*.

Clearly, as this is an average, some businesses will have achieved a multiple below this number and others above it, sometimes well above it. Building a business that is worth many times the average in your sector is more an alchemy than a science. This book will show you how to achieve this alchemy.

It all comes back to the formula contained in this simple diagram. To build a fantastic, asset-rich, wealth-generative business you simply need to build in the right mixture of *people* (talent, capability and culture), *innovation* (of product, system and channel) and *brand*. Understanding this mixture, what each of the ingredients are for your business at each point in its lifecycle, and how and when to blend these, is the secret to creating the *scale* of business and the kind of life you want. That is the purpose of this book.

That's all you to need to know about it for now.

Chapter 2.
The Journey

"*Too many businesses assume that the business they'll have in year five will look pretty much the same as the business they have in year one; there'll just be more people, larger premises, more computing power and so on.*

"*But actually the business can change quite fundamentally over that time and will go through phases of growth where the kind of leadership and management processes might be quite different.*

"*So it's not just a question of getting larger, it's a question of the business having to mature as well.*"

David Molian, Cranfield School of Management

The energetic business story

ABUSINESS, LIKE ANY HUMAN UNDERTAKING, IS A JOURNEY. And it is a journey you do not undertake alone. Rather like my climb up the mountain Aconcagua, building a business involves a complex and evolving set of relationships, hopes, beliefs, joys and disappointments, and moments of euphoria and despair. In a word, it involves energy.

What is truly fascinating is to realise that this energy, these feelings in the business, follows a clear and predictable pattern. Shirlaws – the international business performance company – closely analysed these patterns in thousands of businesses in over 40 countries around the world and from this developed its 'Stages' framework. This is a model of business development that, with remarkable accuracy, can determine where any business is in its lifecycle based purely on the feelings and energy the leadership team articulate.

In many ways this is like a product lifecycle curve. Any product will grow, iterate and eventually decline if left untended. A business is no different.

Knowing where you are in your journey is not only hugely valuable in helping determine priorities and operational activities today but is also a powerful predictive tool to help formulate strategy and planning for the successive stages of the journey.

When you think about it, it's not particularly surprising that how you feel tells you where you are in a cycle – the human experience is remarkably consistent. It's even less surprising that how you feel will predict where you go next. Ask yourself – ask any entrepreneur – how you make decisions and the answer is almost always 'on gut feel'. As Richard Branson says:

> "I rely far more on gut instinct than researching huge amounts of statistics."

If that is the case, then how you feel will immediately and dramatically impact the decisions you make and the confidence and speed with which you make and stick to them.

Stages demonstrates that the stuff you need to do when running a £1m business is different from the stuff you need to do in a £10m business. And the sequence of strategic initiatives to get you from one point to the other evolves over time.

When I said earlier that climbing Aconcagua was all miserable, I was, of course, exaggerating. There were long periods of real joy and shorter periods of very real pain. I felt very different at each stage of the journey. As with climbing a mountain, so with building a business.

Understanding the journey through the powerful and deceptively simple framework called Stages is therefore critical for planning your business journey and understanding which assets you should be focussing on at any one time.

Many CEOs I know (including me) have found it useful to draw the Stages lifecycle on a board or piece of paper and stick it up in their office. It is a great anchor and a powerful reassurance to reflect on your journey so far and help you to plan your future steps. It is also a hugely engaging framework to share with your team.

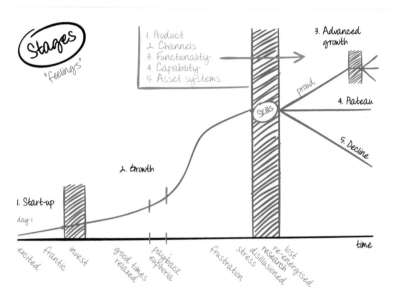

So, let's take a look at the framework and make some sense of it. It shows the stages every business goes through, and grows through, and the dominant feelings or energy the leadership team experience at each of these stages. The timeline has no scale – businesses move through this at very different rates – but the sequence is always the same.

There are five main phases from Start-up through Growth and then on to either Advanced Growth, Plateau or Decline, depending on the choices the leadership team makes at this point. Each business passes along this journey. Where it is on this path is indicated by the predominant energy or feeling in the business from excitement and anxiety at the outset, through a relaxed and even euphoric feeling as things go well, to feelings of frustration and stress. By understanding exactly where you are it is possible to adapt how you run the business to maximise opportunity. It is both a diagnostic and predictive model.

So much for the quick summary. To really understand the framework and how it can serve you in your business journey, you need to experience it as it unfolds step by step.

Be ready to begin the journey

Let's start at the beginning of the journey. It's worth pausing to consider what on earth motivates entrepreneurs to embark on this journey in the first place, with all its attendant risks and rich opportunity for humiliation and financial ruin.

Sometimes it's about the money. But most entrepreneurs are driven by the need to do it for themselves. To quote Simon Sinek, "money is only an end result. Your motivation is more likely freedom." Nick Jenkins states something similar:

> "Why? Freedom, I suppose, more than anything. As a business owner the prospects are unlimited."

For many entrepreneurs, working for someone else is just not a long-term option. Rupert Lee-Browne, Alchemist and CEO of Caxton FX, articulates what a lot of us feel:

> "I think I soon realised that I didn't really like working for other people and other people didn't like me working for them either."

It's reassuring to know that the reasons you started your own business are probably not dissimilar to those of most other entrepreneurs. It's equally reassuring that the journey you embark upon is a well-trodden and predictable path. However, the fact that you are on a predictable journey is no guarantee that you will actually arrive. 20% of businesses fail within the first year and in the next three years a further 50% fail. Sometimes the quality of the idea is just not good enough. Sometimes the entrepreneur has just not done his or her research to really understand the opportunity. But mostly the business is simply starved of cash.

> *"Why do so many businesses fail? They run out of money. It's not a bad idea, it's not bad management, they just run out of money. I would have done that too in the first three years if I hadn't had a bit of cash set aside."*

Nick Jenkins, Moonpig

This book is not about how to start a business. There are many excellent books on that subject. This book is about how to build a mature, wealth-generative, asset-rich business. However, in passing, the advice and experience of the business Alchemists who have travelled this way before is clear:

- Ensure you are as fully funded as possible at the start.

- Do your research so that you understand your business in granular detail.

"Five years planning – five years to feel really ready"

It is remarkable how many of the stories in this book involve the entrepreneur spending two to five years thinking about and planning for their start-up. Looking at the Stages diagram again, it's therefore important to realise that the journey doesn't usually begin at start-up. It actually begins months and often years before that. Nick Jenkins describes his experience of this as follows:

"I went off, did an MBA for a year while I was thinking of a plan and came up with a number of ideas. I had an idea, pulled together a business plan and usually within a week or so worked out why nobody else had done that before or why lots of people had done that before and had failed. Finally I'd narrowed it down to doing something on the internet because it was that time, it was 1998-99, and the internet was coming to the fore."

Most entrepreneurs don't just jump straight into a new business – although increasingly that is exactly what the latest generation of tech-based entrepreneurs do, often in their teens. For the rest of us, we may have been planning for and dreaming of this moment for months or years. The experience of Rupert Lee-Browne of Caxton FX is typical:

"I was never very comfortable being an employee. I think probably the best way to describe it is that when I had accumulated sufficient experience and intelligence to actually make a business work I jumped ship."

For Roger Philby, Alchemist and CEO of The Chemistry Group, the story goes back to 1998 when he was Head of Sales Resourcing for Nortel Networks and became interested in what really drives human potential:

"I was fascinated by working out if I could predict how someone was going to perform and how much was previous experience a predictor of that performance. I wanted to achieve the Holy Grail; hiring more people who perform better and, at the same time, to drive down the cost of hiring. And at Nortel I had an inordinate amount of money, so I engaged clinical psychologists, environmental psychologists, to help me understand human potential. That sowed a seed in me that the way people hire around the planet is wrong.

"I left Nortel in 2001 with the conviction that the data they are using to make the decision on talent is fundamentally flawed. Over the subsequent years I worked on and developed this thinking and the seed planted at Nortel grew into my IP of predicting performance. But I still had a missing thing for me, which was experience of making it work on my own. So I joined a Silicon Valley start-up and I set up Europe for them. I leased offices, I got them furnished, I set up bank accounts, I ran the P&L for Europe, I raised money from VCs. With Nortel and the start-up I was five years planning Chemistry – five years to feel really ready."

It is fascinating to listen to Nick Jenkins when he talks about the focus he had on research and on fully understanding his business model in this pre-start up phase:

"So starting out, I at least knew how to run a business. I'd run a business for Glencore for eight years in Russia, so I knew about hiring people, I knew about pulling teams together, I knew about making things work and I had a little bit of cash. So I thought I'd start with the internet. I looked at the different business models and various ways of making money on the internet. That could have been selling digital content but the problem was that everybody wanted to give it away for free back in 1999, and still that's pretty much the case.

"The other model is offering great content and selling the advertising space around it, but the advertising market online was very embryonic at the time, it would have taken a long time to get off the ground. And it's expensive to pull together really interesting content.

"So, then... what are the other options? Selling physical goods which could be bought in the shops, but if you sell digital cameras online, it was very obvious to me that someone was at some point going to write an algorithm that would compare your price with someone else's price and it's a commodity. If you could buy a Satsuma Fugijitzu 2340 from this dot.com, you're going to buy it from the cheapest one. And ultimately that's going to erode your margins and you've got an enormous amount of money tied up in stock and very low margins so that's a tricky business to be in.

"So then I thought, let's try and find something where you can differentiate the product, and the one point of differentiation is personalisation. So I spent a lot of time looking at things that could be personalised in a way you couldn't do in a shop, so there's no comparison with a shop.

"The one thing I thought of that came back to me again and again, is greeting cards. I used to personalise greeting cards. I'd Tippex out the caption and rewrite my own caption in its place to make it a bit more relevant to the person I'm sending it to. The development of digital printing had made it possible to make a single digital print on cardboard. But, bizarrely, normal household printers will not print on cardboard.

"The element that the internet added was stripping away all the administration. You go to a print shop and ask for a single personalised greeting card it would probably cost you eighty quid by the time you'd done the art work, proofed it and so on and so on, whereas with the internet you basically do everything yourself. And although each individual card is personalised, mechanically they're identical.

"But the other great thing is that you can add a lot of value by personalising a greeting card and by adding good content you can add a lot of value to a piece of paper. So we can take a piece of paper that's worth 3p, add really good content and personalisation, and it's worth £3. You can really make a big difference for a small amount of money so I knew that I was on to a bit of a winner.

"Another benefit is that really the only stock you need is paper and envelopes because the content, although there's a massive amount of content, that's all stored on the server until it gets made so if it doesn't get bought it doesn't get made. And finally, greeting cards go through a letterbox so they can be sent by the Royal Mail which is considerably cheaper than by courier and you don't have to be in when it arrives. As a business model, it's fantastic."

Great businesses can sometimes have the *appearance* of quite casual beginnings. Keith Abel, Alchemist and Founder of Abel & Cole, describes the start of his business like this:

"I think I'd always wanted to run my own business but I didn't have a clue how, but I worked for a guy to earn a few quid at university who had this very simple business buying potatoes, selling them as weekly delivery rounds, a little bit like the milkman. I was just very good at sales; I'd done fire extinguishers when I was sixteen, I'd done life insurance when I was nineteen, I'd learnt from good people and I think I had the right personality – relatively eccentric and outgoing and manic. So I thought, 'Sod it, I'll try doing that in London,' and therefore have my own little business.

"So I bought a ton of potatoes with two mates of mine, and Mum helped out, in Covent Garden market. We bagged them up and sold them in Catford, starting on Firmer Road, for £1.40 a bag. They were costing us 50p to buy, so a very healthy margin, not that I knew what a margin was, I thought that was something on the side of a bit of paper.

"Within three weeks we had a very busy established round and we were out building up another one. We spent £300 on our first van, £250 on our second van and £400 on our third van. So by Christmas we had three vans on the road, we had three van drivers. We were generating cash and we very quickly moved on to getting supplied by a farmer and he was quite happy to have us pay in 60 days, so we had incredibly limited cash requirements. But it was blokes messing about. I'd always intended that I would go and resit my Bar exams in the summer."

Hearing this story from Keith, despite it being related in his modest and self-effacing way, I was struck by that fact that, even here where the founder is suggesting the business was started in the most casual manner, the success of the business was down to the fact that he had done research (tested the idea at university) and understood the core strengths of the model (healthy margin and his own innate selling ability).

A time called Hope

So, however you do it, you cash-up to the extent that is necessary, do your research, gain your experience and your contacts and actually start your business.

This may seem a long time ago but how did you feel on that first day? Excited? A bit nervous? It's a time of high energy – it is the start of a new journey. You may have been planning this for years so to finally get going is bound to be exciting. Finally the day is here. Your business is launched. It is a time of great optimism. A time called *Hope*.

Then, of course, reality strikes. Bills have to be paid, customers won and we have to prove to friends, family and cynics down the pub that we can actually pull this off. We become incredibly busy.

Rupert of Caxton FX says of his early years:

> "I think that in the first years of any business it's about survival and that's a very strong instinct. It's not about grand ideas, it's not about grand plans, it's about 'I've got this business and I'm doing it and my aim is to get success in the next deal, I've got to get through that, and the next one, and I've got to get more clients.'"

This is a time most people remember as frantic. It can be a lot of fun, energy is high, and we are more than willing to put in the long hours. We are still buoyed by hope.

For Russell Stinson at ACT Clean, the start-up phase is indelibly clear – like an episode of *Undercover Boss*.

> "Day one was 26 May 2006. On that day we started a housekeeping contract where we had to clean a 130-bedroom hotel where me, John and Rob [the three founding partners] were up there cleaning the hotel bedrooms personally. It was exciting but ridiculously scary because we weren't the most experienced in housekeeping! We had worked in senior positions in the previous company [Russell had been MD of a large UK support services company] but we took full opportunity to learn it from the ground up. All of us can change the beds, can clean the rooms, can work as floor supervisors, can do the training, can operate the housekeeping system to make sure all the rooms are checked. We had to learn it from the ground up before we could then take on and train

room attendants, floor supervisors and the housekeeping level supervisors. We did it all. It was hard work and it was great fun."

As Russell describes, the first few months or years are often times of anxiety and exceptionally hard work, building the business and winning and servicing clients, hence its description as frantic. Entrepreneurs are full of hope and excitement but there is often a fair amount of anxiety around during this time. Lots of things are tried out in the early months and years and, barring exceptional prescience or luck, not all of them work. It can take time and a lot of energy. Hope's twin sister is called Anxiety!

This period is rarely easy. It requires absolute belief and focus. The Moonpig story is famous for the tenacity with which Nick and his founding team stuck to their guns through a gruelling *five years* of trading loss as they built the business they believed in. Reflecting on it now, Nick says:

> "There were moments when you'd just say 'This isn't working, I'll walk away.' If I could have walked away from Moonpig.com between years two and four, my money intact, I would have done. And that's the bit that a lot of people forget. To be honest, after five years it was a little draining! It was the most extraordinary moment when we finally broke even and you think 'We're going to survive,' because for the first five years it was about survival. What a relief! We're going to survive. We were always within six months of running out of money. Always."

So what kept Nick going? It seems to me the first thing was his absolute belief in the business model based on his clear understanding of its core drivers:

> "We were losing money – year one we had overheads of £1m and sales of £90,000 – but the one thing I could see was that our sales

were rising. That is the thing that kept me going throughout all of that."

And the other factor that leads to perseverance? I think the fear of losing it all – all the cash and all the time and all the energy – keeps us going. As Nick says:

> "I'd made quite a lot of money in Russia and I had put all of it in so if I walked away I had to think pretty hard about what I was going to do next. Actually it's a very important point in terms of business survival because I fought tooth and nail for that business because actually I didn't really have an alternative. One of my investors did say, 'Nick, you can't put any more of your own money into this business because you need something for the next one, and this may not survive.' There's tenacity and there's stubbornness. It's called tenacity if you manage to succeed."

This tenacity to succeed against the odds is what distinguishes entrepreneurs and those with the passion to start a business from those who are content to be an employee. The fear of failure can drive a business like Moonpig to succeed. But it can also compel you to persevere with a business with no hope of success.

I am not alone in having persisted with a business well after the time I should have called it a day, driven by the fear of failure and fear of what I would do next. Proper research at the outset and good advice from those you trust during this period are critical to avoid start-up becoming a road to nowhere and not a pathway to success. Keep in mind the stat I gave earlier – that the majority of businesses fail in their first three years – and occasionally ask yourself and those you trust if your courageous tenacity is actually becoming delusional stubbornness.

Even with proper research, a clear understanding of your business model and adequate funding it is, of course, still bloody hard work.

Roger Philby's experience is typical. With five years of planning under his belt his first client was a significant consulting contract which he used to finance the new business and try things out.

> "I was paid £12,000 a day, which was a lot of money, and I stayed there for 18 months every day of the week apart from weekends, which is how I financed most of the company for a couple of years. I used to get into the client at five o'clock in the morning and turn the lights on and work there until four in the afternoon. Equidistant from my home and the client is Bracknell. So, using a remortgage I started a small office in Bracknell and worked there from 4.30pm, and I started a little recruitment team who were trying to find other clients and work with the IP. I also at the time had created the first video interview technology. So I had consulting, recruitment, and the video proposition... Yes it was frantic!"

The one big thing

Sometimes you suddenly *break through* and start feeling truly confident for the first time. This is not Hope. This is Expectation. On the Stages diagram there is a wall drawn at this point because so many entrepreneurs describe that transition as being like breaking through after months or years of hard work and seeing with absolute clarity and belief for the first time the future growth of their business unfolding before them. So, what did you do? How did you break through that wall? You made an *investment* that changed the rules of the business. This is the First Brick Wall investment.

For Nick Jenkins that First Brick Wall investment is clear and he describes the experience vividly:

> "So, we kept on beavering away and that was just a long, slow path. We've got a good product, the customers love it and

the customers will keep telling their friends about it and we'll keep on growing, which we did. And we grew 30-40% a year in sales until we got through to the point of profitability in 2005 on about £3m worth of sales. And we would have continued to grow steadily and that would have been fine. We had tried all sorts of ways to acquire customers – and that was the key business driver – but there was one thing we hadn't tried yet and that was TV.

"We'd made about £80,000 profit and I'd figured that we could risk that to shift the business. So we spent £80,000 – £30,000 making the ad and £50,000 on media – and we ran a TV campaign about three months later. In my view this is the one thing that we hadn't tried and it worked and it gave us a cost of customer acquisition of £8. And then we doubled it and then we doubled it again, doubled it again, doubled it again. And that's really what turned the business from £3m to £40m turnover in three years."

Listening to Nick, two things stand out for me. The first is that he knew what drove his business model (customer acquisition) and he knew precisely how to measure it (his KPI). In his case he can precisely measure his cost of acquisition. This means he can predict exactly the point that he will breakeven in terms of numbers of customers and can model the date that will occur. Painful though it was, this knowledge supports five years of tenacity and ensures it isn't just stubbornness.

The second is that he tried all sorts of ideas to drive that KPI, most of which were incrementally useful, but there was one big thing that finally shifted the business through the wall and into rapid and sustained growth. It often isn't clear beforehand what this investment will be, so it is critical to keep innovating and trying new things in this period.

Keith Abel describes how, after years of struggling with a complex paper-based order system, he invested in both a website and integrated CRM package that transformed the business overnight.

"Five years in, we're selling huge amounts of potatoes, huge amounts of eggs and we're starting to do these boxes of organic veg. We've got loads and loads of vans and very poor financial controls. At that point, introducing IT systems was crucial for our business as you can imagine. It was a nightmare, an absolute nightmare. You'd arrive in the morning, there'd be 30 messages on the answering machine, it would take you four hours to clear them. If someone told you their address you had to flick through an A-Z, find out the grid reference, go to a big map on the wall which we'd laminated, go up the grid reference from one side to the other and then in that circle it would say 'Tuesday Round 8'. And you'd go and find Tuesday Round 8's book and you'd flick through it and there would be that customer, and they were just asking for an extra half a dozen eggs.

"People didn't have computers in the '90s, this was the very beginnings of spreadsheets and things. But we realised there was no way we'd be able to grow without it. We were collecting cash from the customers at the time so the controls were incredibly difficult. So we went through a phase of getting it all on to a database and building a transactional website. So that helped enormously."

The First Brick Wall investment can be in staff, systems, plant, acquisitions, advice, perhaps even taking yourself off on a business or personal development course – something that releases the energy, creativity and talent of the founding team to focus on growth. For Russell Stinson that initial investment was in a talented team. That initial team of three friends and business partners cleaning hotel bedrooms in London were able to scale but had a skills gap in Operations. Russell explains how the fourth partner came on board:

"Paul had been a client, someone we had known, someone very experienced in London's five-star hospitality sector. I think we very quickly realised the value of Paul's skill set, his work ethic and his determination to really make this work."

Bringing Paul into this established business was "a bit of a no brainer." But in bringing Paul in, the investment the original trio made was significant; both commercially and culturally. Despite the risk taken and sweat expended, they chose to make Paul an equal partner. Russell Stinson says:

"We talked about a percentage, sure, but, whenever we took a much closer look at it, it looked much better as an equal partnership between four. I think Paul would tell you himself he wasn't expecting this but he massively appreciated it and I think it gave us all a real focus where we knew our individual skills sets – John in business development, Rob in legal, compliance, HR, training and that side of it, myself in the business, finance, systems side of it and Paul the operations side of it. This gave us a real balanced skill set across a company structure and architecture where there weren't really any gaps. And I think that allowed us to grow rapidly in those first few years."

For Roger Philby, breaking through the First Wall and moving on to the rapid growth that followed was equally clear, in the form of two key investments:

"It took off like a train so we were a company that was quite good at something and all of a sudden we were billing two million quid by the end of the first full year.

"The first investment was the model, the five years' worth of investment, which I don't think has ever been written on a balance sheet. And the second was hiring Lorraine because it went gangbusters after she joined and it wouldn't have done without her simply because I couldn't have leveraged myself."

Some businesses, of course, never break through that wall. They never find that first significant investment. They are stuck in a perpetual repetitive cycle. They may create reasonable revenues and profit but they will never reach their potential. They may even make it to £1m and get stuck. They will never achieve scale.

This can be perfectly satisfactory. However, if the founder's ambitions are greater it can create constant anxiety and franticness; a feeling of being stuck on a hamster wheel. To get off the wheel and break through, the business has to find and make an investment; the owners need to detach from what they have been doing and attach to something new – even if that is just new thinking. Even if that is simply belief. This investment can be impossible to find without the benefit of some perspective.

If this resonates with you then perhaps it's time to get advice and help for your business.

Confidence becomes the norm

Once on the other side of that wall, how do you feel? Relaxed. Confidence has become the norm – you know this is going to work. You are still very busy and it can involve you putting in long hours but your business feels like it is in flow – your product is simple but it is clear, your customers understand what you do and want to buy it, your team are aligned and having fun.

Your focus in this period is still very much outward: winning new clients, developing and finessing your product. Internal systems can be fairly threadbare but it doesn't seem to matter. No one minds working hard and making do. In fact, businesses in this phase tend to believe in *work hard, play hard*. It may feel like you are all working long hours but you still make time for having a good time together as a team – company trips are common and the Christmas party becomes legendary.

Having a blast

With this aligned energy the business grows. Every month is better than the last, every customer is bigger than the last. This is a good time. In the future, you will look back on this and call it the good old days.

> *"Suddenly I'm flying around the world being really successful, getting a bit of a name... It was a blast. We picked up bigger and bigger projects. We were up at 26 employees, revenues of £250,000 a month. "*

Roger Philby

What goes wrong? Nothing. What could? You are the master of your universe. It's payback time for all those hours of graft and you feel amazing. You start to look at how all your hard work can reward you and the key team who started with you. You upgrade your lifestyles – the second home, that DB9, boats, school fees – you deserve it after all. And time. You've worked really hard for years and you need time for yourself. Time on the boat and at that second home.

Accelerated growing pains

The business is growing faster than ever and, if your eye is not firmly on the ball things can get out of control. Keith Abel describes this rapid growth phase of Abel & Cole like this:

> "So 2002-2007 were major boom times, we went 3, 6, 13, 19, 28 million pounds in turnover and you've got to be much more fussed about the infrastructure. It's bloody difficult growing a business that fast; getting more warehouse space, getting more management, getting more teams... nightmare, nightmare stuff."

This focus on more – more stuff, more people – is familiar to any business owner who has moved through the Accelerated Growth phase. Money is flooding in but you need new people to support that growth (possibly new management to support your new lifestyle). Costs begin to creep up, margins are squeezed.

An entrepreneur once described to me that he knew when his business was in payback when the CFO said, "we made £1m revenues this month," and they celebrated. And he knew they were *out* of payback when the CFO said, "you guys need to make £1m revenues this month to hit our numbers."

Russell Stinson of ACT Clean puts it like this:

> "The level of growth is still rapid but we're now realising that we need to change because it's not been a smooth ride to 1300 staff. We're adding significant growth, winning 75% of new openings of hotels and restaurants in the four and five star market, and we've got to bring in more and more skilled and talented people – many from outside our industry. We've got to get the systems right to cope with it. Plus there's a much bigger focus on compliance across health and safety and from an employment point of view.

"We've had to develop the systems to cope with all of that and you could see the amount of spaghetti that was starting to be generated within the business, that there wasn't a real clarity of who was responsible for which role so we're starting to get frustrated, so bringing much greater clarity to people's roles and what's expected of them has been essential."

As Russell describes, this can then be a gradual process of building frustration. The business is still growing but to you it feels increasingly out of control. That *flow* you had in good times has gone. This business is complicated. There are more people involved. And they don't seem to get it and get you like your team in the early days.

Your frustration turns to stress. You are working longer hours to try and keep the thing on the rails. You are fighting fires – getting involved in all sorts of operational problems that sap your energy. You don't see the kids as much as you did or should. You argue with your spouse. You get ill.

A whole world of horribleness

At this point you smash into that Second Brick Wall. You are thoroughly disillusioned. What do you do?

Let's look at Frank Bastow's experience:

"When I was a kid I just went, 'Oh, I'll go and work for the old man until I get myself sorted out.' So I did just that and rapidly became worker, site foreman, contracts manager... and then ended up becoming managing director before I knew what I was doing. Then in '92, I said to the old man, 'Tell me, when am I going to run this business, when am I going to be in charge?' I remember his answer to this day. He said to me, 'As long as I'm fucking alive you'll never run this fucking business.' So I said, 'Well, I'm off.' He replied, 'Take whoever you like and sod off and go.'

"So I started off with a few people and I set up offices in Fulham. And from 1992-2000, I built a business called Tremayne. I built my own universe – made it the way I wanted my workers and my clients to be – and I was turning over about £900,000 a year with 12 guys. Then my Dad rang me up and said, 'Can we do a deal on Bastows?' I bought Bastows up lock, stock and barrel, thinking that the culture was going to be exactly the same as my own new business. I had this romantic idea; I wanted the Bastow name back.

"And we had some good years. Instead of being offered a maximum of a quarter of a million pound jobs, I was getting offered one million pound jobs. That felt pretty good. But the cultural differences in the two firms were never sorted out and it all went bad. We had our first bad year in 2005, I think it was, and that's when it went all pear-shaped with the old man, and he left. That was the Second Wall for me – when the culture clashed and people were fighting and forming camps: 'You're Tremayne'...'You're Bastows'. It was a nightmare!"

For some, the Second Brick Wall is so painful and apparently insoluble that they give up – or sell out at a fraction of the value of what their stake is worth. But most entrepreneurs are fighters, so they look for solutions, hire new management, go on a course, hire a NED or coach. But like the First Wall, unless you invest in the right things you can just stay there, circulating around in stress and disillusionment, plateauing or in decline.

Roger Philby says this about the situation:

"We might have been growing fast and got our positioning bang on, but the big problem was our platform – we hadn't done any planning for growth, we'd just grown. I just didn't know. I was heady with it. Yes, it was a fun place to be but only because we had a PlayStation – there was nothing conscious about the culture. We hadn't stuck to our own principles around hiring so I'd hired a bunch of people on quite big salaries. We didn't talk about values, we were just kind of getting on with it. I was doing a lot of travelling and I wasn't paying a lot of attention.

"I remember coming back from the US and Lorraine sits me down and says, 'We've got no money.' And I said, 'What do you mean we don't have money? We've just billed £300,000, of course we've got money. I'm working my arse off round the world to generate revenue.'

"'Yeah, but the cost base has grown to X.'

"'What?! No, it's not. We've hired a few...' and it sounds really naive and really stupid sat here now ten years later. At the time, genuinely, and I'm sure people who read this will think he's an idiot, but genuinely it didn't occur. Then, I go and see the accountant who says, 'You're in shit,' and I go, 'Yeah. I picked that up.'

"'No, he says, I don't mean that. You haven't paid PAYE for 18 months.' Long pause.

"Basically, somewhere between his accountancy firm and my guys, an administrator had changed and no one had picked up cheques stopped going to PAYE. So now I've got a business that's not generating any profit and we owe PAYE three or four hundred thousand pounds. So I initiated something called Project Phoenix to return the company to profitability and I did things I've never done before. I fired ten people. Just walked into the office and said you're going to have to go."

This is the Second Brick Wall. And it can go on for years. It can become your life. I remember a CEO telling me about the day he dropped his daughter off at university for the first time. As he pulled away and looked at her diminishing in his rear view mirror he had a sudden realisation:

> "I realised that I really didn't know this girl. That for most of her life I had been so overwhelmed by my business that I had allowed my relationship with her to take second place. And that for the last several critical years I had hardly been there at all. And I had this sick, sick realisation that it was now just too damn late."

Continuing the story from The Chemistry Group, Roger Philby says:

> "So I wound the business in but then didn't do any of the platform things that I should have done. I actually returned the business to profitability and I wasn't depressed, I was motivated to try again. And we got it back profitable again and I started paying PAYE but the £400,000 in charges was still there. So I struggled on. We wound it down, started to build it up again. The cash flow was driving all the decision-making. We convinced ourselves that we were running the business properly which was not true because what we couldn't do was grow. We'd hit a sort of brick wall.

> "I hired some people in and we did some different things and we created a consultancy brand which in the end died. And every time we tried to grow we had to wind it back in again. And all the time we had this big debt. I started to get depressed. I just couldn't work out what was stopping me. I just had this horrific sense that five years' worth of remortgage and hard work and all of that stuff had just gone to pot. My behaviour started changing, a whole world of horribleness."

At the stage of the Second Brick Wall nothing you try seems to work, the joy has gone out of the business and your life. To escape from this world of horribleness what you need, once again, is a different kind of business – a business with new skills, capabilities and platforms.

Frank Bastow describes it like this:

> "So, I've got all this infighting and grief, and the business isn't going anywhere. I'd had enough. I said, 'We're all the same, all the same company.' We needed alignment. That's when we moved the whole lot over to Kingston and immediately had a fresh energy. That's when I started to work with the Shirlaws models. I got rid of some people, and some people saw how we were working and they jumped ship. I lost all the old office staff within three months. But until we sorted out our intent and what our positioning was... well, that was the most painful thing. That's what I tell everybody; functionality, capability, capacity... they're really easy if you know what your intent and your positioning is."

To break through this second wall required Roger Philby to think about things differently:

> "I wasn't really listening to anyone, it was just such a horrific time, I was grieving. And then one day I was shown the Shirlaws capacity model. And I kind of went, 'Wow, now I understand the difference between growth and platform. The reason that I've never grown is all I've ever done is growth strategy.' And then I was shown Shirlaws model for functionality. Oh my god! If I put functionality with capacity! And then I did probably the hardest thing I've ever had to do which was to pull the entire company together and told them the truth about the business and how I needed their help. So they all agreed to cut their salary on the

basis that if the business achieved a particular level we would pay it back. They only had to take the cut for two months."

Focus on the five skills

To get clear of the Second Brick Wall, you need to invest in a fundamentally different kind of business. A business with new skills. One that is able to focus on the development of its assets and not just manage its profit. A business that focuses on both 'P' and 'M'. A business that can be said to be in advanced growth.

Roger Philby puts it like this:

> "So first we got our platform in place using functionality and capacity strategies [see Chapter 3]. We realised we had a strong product, a strong position and I knew that if people experienced my team they always bought again. We had a client roster that most organisations would die for. We had assets and we realised we wanted a different kind of business. We started looking at culture and we said, 'Look, you know, we think we've got a great culture but we've never described it to anyone else, it's not really sustained so it's patchy.' So we worked on that. We knew our product was great but confused and in some areas lacked differentiation so we took the brave decision to get out of recruitment overnight to create focus. And then we built our way up the valuation framework to the business we have today."

What Roger's story articulates is that you need to invest and seriously focus on a small number of fundamental skills to pass through this Second Brick Wall and truly into advanced (asset) growth. There are five fundamental skills and they can be simplified as follows:

1. Product

Your business needs a clear and distinct product (in which I include service) or set of products. These are distinct from your competition because your products are positioned with a unique brand architecture that makes them different, relevant and creates cut-through in your marketplace. Part of the work to get through the Second Brick Wall is to strengthen internal systems to productise and innovate on an ongoing basis in order to adapt to changing markets and achieve a sustainable business.

2. Channels

You need to develop and fully exploit your channels to market to promote and distribute your product, providing a consistent and scalable flow of clients and revenue. Very often growth tends to slow or stall prior to/during the Second Brick Wall because the marketplace that previously served the business so well has become less attractive (either saturated or being served by new competition). The business needs to develop new, and probably multiple, routes to market ensuring a consistent flow of clients and revenue.

3. Functionality

A functional internal structure ensures the right people are doing the right jobs at the right times. This is most critical at the Second Brick Wall stage because enough capacity has to be created in the senior team to spend in strategy activity to make sure the right choices are made and assets are built to access advanced growth.

4. Capability

As the business identifies new revenue strategies (products and channels) it will need to build new capability. Together with functionality, this is the core building block of your management system to ensure the business is able to reinvent itself successfully. Often it is critical to fix the management systems before the business is able to invest productively in revenue and asset systems.

5. Asset Systems

Finally, you must have understood and defined all the key asset drivers in your business – the assets that impact the *equity value* of the business. Then you can start to develop and build these. When a business has developed an asset system it has gained the ability to leverage core capabilities so that assets are driving new business opportunities. This unlocks a transition from running a single P&L business (prior to the Second Brick Wall), to running a portfolio of business assets – possibly separate businesses which are extensions of core assets – into new markets. This is the prerequisite for advanced growth and enhanced value. In other words you need to be working on the multiple, not just the profit.

The Abel & Cole story is a real demonstration of this process in action. When we last heard from Keith Abel's story the business was in rapid growth through £28m turnover in 2007 – at which point Keith accepted a generous offer and sold the business to private equity. Yet within two years the business was in serious trouble and Keith, famously, was brought back in and turned things around dramatically before the business was sold again for "an undisclosed sum" in 2012 with turnover at £55m.

So what went wrong – and how did Keith turn it round? When we spoke, Keith was at pains to point out that the new management were far from incompetent. "They were bright people," he says. "It's funny. A little tampering with the basic idea just put the business in freefall." To understand what this 'little tampering' amounted to, it is worth exploring the story. Keep in mind the five skills above as you read.

The Alchemist's view

In conversation with Keith Abel

Keith, it is 2007. The business is growing fast, passing £28m, and you sell to private equity. Tell me what happened next. I guess a major part of this is that the recession happened?

"Yes. Terrible timing for them. The financial crisis starts and inevitably growth isn't what was predicted. Quite understandably they start missing their business plan, only very slightly, and they need to take action. The trouble is that their response was to be more like a supermarket, putting pressure on our suppliers to give us the best price and the focus wasn't on the best quality. The focus moved to discounting to our consumer and into new ideas.

"In any good business focusing on doing it well and doing it better and better is usually the best response to a crisis. If you've got a really good business just make what you are doing now better. I can go and find at least five things that we can do better with what we've got and that we know works. Under all that pressure I think that absolute focus slipped. The focus on what Abel & Cole did brilliantly – as a bit quirky but delivering a really good veg box – slipped. I think a lot of management teams forget what made the business famous and they forget to ask the customer what they actually want – what the experience is. I can go to any business and make it better by five things. There are always five things you can find to make it better. That is how brilliant businesses are made. It's just unbelievable attention to detail."

A focus on the core Product and what you are famous for is key?

"Yes. That and how you get to market."

Can I call that your Channel?

"It's important to understand not just what your customer buys but how they like to buy it."

The functional structure of the business can become somewhat confused and inefficient?

"Yes, if you don't watch it. And the risk is that you then don't pay enough attention to detail and the business can start looking a bit shabby round the edges. A lot of companies, as they grow, start bringing in people – often too many expensive people from big corporate backgrounds who look good on paper but don't quite 'get' your business."

Is this about management capability? Or an effective management system?

"In our case it was nothing to do with the quality of the senior team. They were an extremely bright bunch of people who'd had an awful lot of success in the past. It was a terribly difficult time in the economy and I think with all that going on it's easy to just lose track of what the real drivers in the business are.

"What I say to people when they're in a downturn or business is in a bit of a crisis, is: 'Don't lose your nerve, think about what you stand for, don't start putting 50% off your Aston Martin, just try and improve the bloody thing so that it's so completely fantastic that anyone who's a potential buyer becomes a buyer.'"

You're saying stick to your five things. Whatever they are, the five things you need to improve. Understand the core rocket fuel, the thing that my business stands for and believes in, the things that people buy?

"Yes, so now I'll tell you what we did do when we went back which was two years later. We got together, Ted (the MD) and I, and spoke to lots of people who I trusted within the business. I had been having a delivery at home myself and knew that it was all looking very shabby. My attitude was, well, if we're going to go bust, let's just do it with a smile on our faces. Let's just make sure that we do the best product we've ever done.

"And there was terribly low morale because everyone was being laid off and you always think 'It's going to be me next.' So we very quickly had this rough idea of what we wanted to do, but instead of imposing it on everyone else we invited everyone who worked in the business to come to my house in five groups to discuss what they'd like to do with the business, and we called them different projects.

"We had Project Shuffle, which was that everyone in their office or their workplace was going to move or change something. We had Project Kindness, which was we were going to find ways that our business could help people in the local community a bit more. We had Project Product, which was what we were going to do to improve the product, etc.

"We were at about 240 employees at that time and 125 volunteered to come here on five separate days, and I made lots of tea and cakes. I just said, 'It's great for you lot to be here and what you've got to say is just as important as what Ted or I have to say.' And the deal was that Ted and I tried as much as possible to shut up. We said, 'Just come up with five things that you think we could improve on,' in each project. Then we might have 200 ideas written up on sheets of paper all around the walls.

"Then we broke up into five groups and one would go into the dining room, one would go in here, one would go in the hallway and they would discuss those five things and then they'd come back with what they thought were the very best ideas that were coming out of that day. And you could guarantee that whatever Ted and I thought was the most important idea of the day was always in that group, and on top of it there would be things we would never have thought of. And then we'd say, 'Brilliant guys, that's what we're going to do.' So it was no longer our ideas, it was their ideas, and they'd go back into work and go 'It's brilliant, you know we've been saying we wanted to do that for ages.'

"Then Ted and I went on a massive tour of the country. We went to every single depot and we'd get there at 3am and cook them breakfast. And we'd just assure them that we were going to listen to everything they had to say about what we could do to improve things.

"They'd say things like 'Look, we appreciate that times are tough and we've got a shitty van but I haven't had a radio in my van for three weeks and I'm being told we can't afford it.' And we'd go 'Right, that's not reasonable, you're having a radio in your van and it's going to be there tomorrow.' There was one depot we went to and the loos were just shocking. For a thousand quid we got new loos installed. Can you imagine what that felt like to be a driver there?

"We just said we're going to do that for you, whatever you ask, and we're here to cook you breakfast. And you've got to go to every customer with a massive smile on your face, you've got to listen to any feedback, you've got to do what you're asked by customer service, you've got to collect the boxes, you've got to do it with a smile, you've got to give us 120% and if it doesn't work we're going to go bust feeling proud. And so, of course, everyone starts doing their job better. Suddenly we had a brilliant product. Within three weeks we had a transformed product."

What else did you do with the product?

"We bought much better. We focussed. So we went from 3000 SKUs [unique stock items] to 800. We spent much more money on the box. We ignored margin. We packaged potatoes into a nice little brown paper bag. We put a recipe on the side of the bag. We told them on the other side of the bag who grew it, where it was from and it was all a bit quirky. We put dividers in the boxes so that the product was held upright, rather than all sagging around and rolling all over the place. We put the muddy stuff in one of the divides, we put the other stuff in the other divide.

"To save money the previous incumbents had string-tied the boxes only one way so they didn't look like a parcel. We immediately implemented double-string tying so they all looked much more pukkah. We chucked out any slightly damaged boxes 'coz they were recycling these boxes that shouldn't have been used again, they had stains in the bottom and we went, 'No, this is a premium product, it's bloody well going to look better than it did'."

And on functionality and the management system?

"Everyone's office moved. And when they did we put a lick of paint on the wall. We got new chairs for people in customer services 'coz their chairs were broken and they were getting bad backs. We got the showers fixed. But the amounts of money we were spending were relatively small. We probably spent sort of £50,000 in total on really transforming the way that the whole work place looked and felt.

"We reorganised the marketing team. So we suddenly went from a team of about 12 and three external agencies to no external agencies and two people. So in April-May, we significantly improved the product. June, we put the prices up by 5%. No one even flinched because for a month they'd been getting the best product they'd ever had."

And then?

"And then we did an absolutely massive and incredibly bold marketing campaign and it worked. We went from £27m to £55m in two years."

Lessons from Abel & Cole

What do the lessons from Abel & Cole demonstrate?

Particularly, to pass through the Second Brick Wall you need real focus on five things. You need to have an absolute focus on a clearly articulated **product** and obsess about making it the best it can be by asking staff and, above all, customers.

You need to fully manage your **channel** and make sure it's right for the business at this point in the cycle. You need a **functional** system and platform to support it all. And proper and motivated management **capability** such that all this is operationally independent of you to allow you and your key team to focus on defining and building the **assets** that turn your business from a good, profit-generating concern into a truly great asset-based wealth generator.

Reviewing that list of key skills again, in many ways the first four – Product, Channels, Functionality, Capability – really allow for the last, and most important, Asset Systems, to happen.

And what is beyond the Second Brick Wall? What does it feel like to run a business in the Advanced Growth stage? You have built a business that will thrive beyond your direct involvement and according to most CEOs I meet, the feeling they have is pride. It's a humble pride but a deep, systemic pride from having moved through the lifecycle, faced the challenges, built something worthwhile for the family at work and the family at home. And lived to tell the tale.

Frank Bastow's experience of creating a genuinely functional and systemised business was that his role changed dramatically:

"All I do now is coach my team. They run everything in the business. Which gives me all the time in the world to create new businesses."

Frank now has four additional businesses, none in the building sector but all based on the assets he developed in the original business.

"I met this fella yesterday and he asked me what I did. I told him: 'I run five businesses; I'm moving into a house I built which is all totally green. I've just got the planning permission for two houses on my existing property; I'm going to Las Vegas for five days to play the veteran Poker World Series; and I've got a walk which I'm going to have to start training for when I come back from Las Vegas – because I'm 18 stone and I've got to walk 100 kilometres in twenty four hours'. And this guy says, 'Blimey, you must be busy.' And I say, 'I'm not busy. I've got all the time in the world. I have my capacity sorted out and every day I've got all the time in the world.'"

That is how it feels to run an advanced growth, asset-focussed business.

Of course, that is not the experience of every business. Not everyone running a business will have this experience as Roger and Frank have described it. For a start, payback in the midst of the biggest economic downturn for at least a generation is inevitably going to be somewhat muted. Your payback might just be that your business survives.

Your experience of the Second Brick Wall depends on the skills, platforms and assets you have built as you ran up the growth curve. In talking to Russell Stinson of ACT Clean it's clear that the experience the senior team had previously gained in running entrepreneurial businesses, twinned with their tight and aligned partnership, saw them putting into the business a lot of the skills needed to pass through the Second Brick Wall well in advance of serious stress developing. Russell explains:

> "We brought in a hugely experienced finance director quite early so my need to spend time in finance is virtually zero. And that has been the pattern: to recruit quality people. We had an HR director come in who's got huge experience across hospitality, taking a huge weight off Rob. Then we brought in an operations director with vast experience that took a huge responsibility off Paul. But because of the growth doubling in size the operational challenge is just an ongoing one and I think that's where we've needed to get the culture right, the training right, the development right, the succession planning right. All this is absolutely key to run an operation where on a weekly basis we've got 1300 staff working."

All businesses are likely to have developed bits of all the skills detailed in the Stages drawing. That's not good enough. To truly move through that wall and into the kind of advanced-growth business the Alchemists enjoy, the kind of business that is highly valued, your strategy must be *fully* implemented at *every* level.

And most fundamentally of all, you must have built resources and systems to allow everything else to flow. Without these in place you don't even make it on to the Seven Layers of Valuation. You are not yet at benchmark. We'll look at that in the next chapter.

Action plan: Ten things to do now

1. **Take a look at your Stages journey. Draw the model.** Where is your business today? Where are you personally? And where are your key team? What is coming up?

2. **Hold a strategic retreat offsite, ideally once per quarter**. Include an exploration of Stages with your key team in your next retreat.

3. Decide specifically what you need to do to **effectively navigate through the next stage**.

4. If one of your businesses is in start-up **make sure you fully understand the sector, drivers and the KPIs against which you'll measure success**. Ensure that your tenacity is not becoming stubbornness.

5. If you feel the business is ready to shift into sustained growth, work out what investment will create that shift. **What is your one big thing? What do you need to invest in commercially and energetically?** What must you detach from and attach to even if it's just in your head?

6. If your business is in sustained growth, **invest early in the five key skills**.

7. Make sure you **have an absolute focus on what makes you famous**. Obsess about making it the best it can be from a customer's perspective. Listen to your people, talk to your customers and become a customer if you can.

8. **Make sure your channel strategy is right for the business** at this point in your business lifecycle and for the economy.

9. Invest time and focus in your **functional system and platform**.

10. **Ensure you have full capability in your management team**. Train generously. Don't be sentimental if it's time for someone to move on.

Chapter 3.
Excellent is Good Enough

"So much of what we call management consists in making it difficult for people to work."

Peter Drucker

Getting to benchmark

V+7	Scale
V+6	Brand architecture
V+5	Channel extension
V+4	Product extension
V+3	Systems / product innovation
V+2	Talent / capability / culture
V1	Industry benchmark
V-2	Cost management
V-3	Revenue management
V-4	Asset management
V-5	Liability management
V-6	Quality management team
V-7	Economic / Political / Consumer section risks

IN THE PREVIOUS CHAPTER I SAID THAT YOU NEEDED FIVE KEY areas of focus to get through that Second Wall and become a truly asset-focussed, advanced-growth business. This is all about creating a platform that will allow your business to scale beyond your ability to directly manage it.

To quote Alastair Lukies, CEO of Monitise:

> "Building a business is very much like a pyramid. Too many people focus on the top of the pyramid but don't spend enough time on what is inevitably the dull but essential stuff which is 'How do I build the bottom of the pyramid so robustly and so scalably that if my strategy changes it's only a tweak at the bottom to make it happen?'"

The purpose of this chapter is to introduce that dull stuff.

Fundamentally damaging to your wealth

The dull stuff, if done badly, is what can undermine your business value and prevent you achieving even a benchmark valuation. It's the basics any valuer, funder or partner will expect to see reliably and credibly in place in your business. It includes how you manage costs and deliver revenue, what the assets and liabilities on your balance sheet look like, and if your management team is up to scratch. If you have already put a big tick against each of these you will find much of this chapter irrelevant so feel free to skip through. If not, it's pretty critical you get these right before you embark on your asset journey.

It is not the function of this book to get into huge depth around these topics. Our purpose here is to look at what builds a great, asset-rich business. However, before we get there we need to at least acknowledge the vital importance of the platform upon which all of that growth and wealth is built.

If you are looking for more support I think a great and very thorough book to dip into is *From Vision to Exit* by Guy Rigby. Guy is a highly regarded Chartered Accountant and partner at Smith & Williamson, a firm well known in the entrepreneurial space. Guy is also a seasoned entrepreneur in his own right. You will see that I have borrowed liberally from his book in this chapter. I would highly recommend getting a hold of a copy for more detail on these topics.

Let's start by looking at my list of five key skills again but in a slightly different order, so that we take a look at costs first before moving on to revenue and finally assets:

1. **Functionality**. The right people doing the right jobs at the right time with systems and capacity deployed to ensure you have an efficient and scalable platform, independent of senior management.

2. **Product**. A clear and distinct product with a unique positioning that makes it different, relevant and creates cut-through in your marketplace.

3. **Channels to market**. To promote and distribute your product, providing a consistent and scalable flow of clients and revenue.

4. **Capability**. A truly capable management team and the ability to track capability and performance of the team and business.

5. **Asset Systems**. A defined set of key asset drivers in your business so as to be working on the multiple not just the profit.

Looking at this list you'll observe that (1) is all about your systems of cost management, (2) and (3) are about your systems of revenue creation and (4) is about the quality of your management systems. These are the key variables of your business platform upon which you will then build your asset pyramid (5).

They are also the key factors that can depress your asset value. If you don't get these right, your business won't even command a multiple of earnings that is average in your sector. That average multiple is referred to as the *benchmark value* in your industry and to achieve that a valuer will assume you have your costs, revenues and management working effectively. Not getting this right is therefore fundamentally damaging to your wealth. And it will absolutely prevent you from building the high-value, joy-to-own business you want.

Here is a conundrum:

- I fundamentally believe that those who own and run businesses who focus solely on profit (costs and revenues) keep their business small and get stuck on the hamster wheel I referred to in the previous chapter. Without a sense of assets and not just revenue, multiple and not just profit, why and not just how, business owners don't invest, don't grow and don't break through walls.

- And yet *without* this focus you can't build the platform you need to scale up your business.

So how to resolve that dilemma? Clearly it's a matter of timing – it depends on what Stage you are at in the business cycle.

Focus on your platform first, get the fundamentals right, with the *absolute intention* of it becoming systemised and wholly independent of you. It is too easy to get stuck in the operations of your business. After all, you built it. You may be good at it but it's not the best use of your personal assets. So, in this chapter, let's focus on building that platform. And then in the rest of the book we'll look at how to build a pyramid of assets.

Cash is king

In *From Vision to Exit* Guy Rigby makes the point that "businesses don't go bust because of a lack of profitability. They go bust because they run out of cash." This was the experience of Roger Philby, of the Chemistry Group, when his profitable business with a £3m turnover ran out of cash.

The source of the problem was a lack of cost management systems. As Roger explained in the previous chapter, "so I wound the business in but then didn't do any of the platform things that I should have done."

To quote Guy in more depth:

> "A business that doesn't understand its financial position is flying blind. It's amazing how often it occurs. Such a business generally has no basis on which to make decisions, no ability to commit a future investment and no understanding of what activity or issue will eventually cause it to fail, apart from the inevitable absence of cash. Sometimes this results from an accounting breakdown, a people or systems failure and sometimes, perhaps most frequently, it arises because of a lack of understanding of the critical importance of the finance function resulting in under under-resourcing or the employment of unqualified staff or both."

Giles Murphy, head of assurance and business services at Smith & Williamson, makes the point that "fundamentally a business must be able to understand and monitor its financial dynamics."

Monitoring and measurement is critical. Apart from anything else it helps you keep a tight control over costs.

Cost management

It is obviously important to keep direct and indirect costs under control – and under review – at all times. It's vital to understand the complete cost structure of the business, including hidden costs and costs we become blind to. Ajaz Ahmed, founder of a complex and international business, is clear that "watching costs like a hawk is absolutely essential however big the company is. That comes right from the top. From the leaders."

It's therefore obviously a good idea to regularly review all your supplier arrangements and seek out better and cheaper ways of doing things.

What interests us here is not so much the actual cost structure of your business. Vital though that is, it sits in a *profit* box and we are interested in building assets. We are therefore more interested in the *systems* of cost management rather than the costs themselves. It's a circular argument, of course, because putting in the right systems necessarily reduces your costs. It is, however, a matter of focus. I want to look at the source of cost management (the system) and not the outcome (better productivity). I want to look at the context not the content.

It's also obvious that having the CEO actively managing all this is frustrating and unsustainable. The CEO's job is to set context and priorities, create a culture of efficiency and innovation, ensure robust systems are in place and *move on*.

For most businesses the key area of cost is, of course, people. As I explore in the next chapter, people represent both a major cost and a massive asset to the business. To build your pyramid any higher it is clearly critical to build a platform of aligned, committed and high-performing people. This is about creating the right culture (see Chapter 4). But is also about creating *systems* that allow that culture of efficiency and performance to develop and be effectively deployed.

How often do the leadership team find themselves spending time handling day-to-day tasks and fire-fighting myriad issues that constantly arise in an SME? These issues can and should be handled by other people in the business.

The cost to this is not just to your youthful good looks. It also prevents you from growing the assets – both cultural and commercial – that will turn the good business into something truly great.

Every job is only done once

The problem is that, more often than not, in a company that has grown from the top down, owners structure their businesses without a real plan in mind. As the business expands, they simply hire staff. Businesses don't grow in an orderly, methodical way. Growth turns up in lumpy chunks and the key to your success is how you create a *system* to manage those chunks.

If you're serious about growing your business, *resourcing* should be a strategic function. The starting point is to identify the best functional structure for your business, one that will enable you to step back from a fully operational role, maximise the talents of your employees, significantly reduce operating costs and consequently operate at maximum profitability.

This means assessing which job functions and activities are really needed and then allocating roles to the people who are most appropriately skilled or experienced for those jobs. You may well find that the most appropriate person is located in another part of the business, or you might have to bring in some training to develop a skill the business needs.

Red, blue and black

The trick is to create a structure or system that allows that talent to emerge and for the business to leverage its people in an optimal way; a system that creates a truly functional business. One example of this that I have seen to work time and time again is the Shirlaws system of dividing business activities within an organisation into three groups and colour coding them as red, blue or black activities. As a simple way to start to systemise a business's functions it is as neat as any I've seen.

By using a simple system like this you can easily plot where time is currently spent across your business and then match that against what the business actually needs. In your business:

- Red activities are those that support the infrastructure and are non-revenue-generating, such as administration, finance, HR and IT.

- **Blue activities** are all revenue-generating functions and are customer related, so include anything to do with making, selling, delivering and servicing whatever your customers buy from you – as well anyone involved in marketing, for example.

- **Black activities** include any functions related to business growth. These include leadership functions such as the development and nurturing of culture and setting of the vision, as well as other contextual areas that will create long-term growth such as developing your market positioning, new product and packaging strategies, key external professional and referral relationships, and joint venture, licensing or merger activity (in other words building your assets).

The diagram below illustrates the colour-coded model for the three areas of business.

Red, Blue, Black

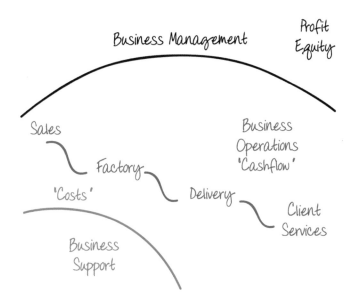

Business Management

Profit
Equity

Sales

Business
Operations
'Cashflow'

Factory

'Costs'

Delivery

Client
Services

Business
Support

Too often business owners and directors are busy handling red and blue activities instead of strategic black activities. Sorting out IT problems, organising for the offices to be decorated, handling a stock problem or even doing sales calls because you believe customers like to see the boss are not black or strategic functions – so you should not be spending time on them.

Start with yourself. For most of us it's a salutary exercise to systematically (and honestly!) colour-code a typical week in red, blue and black. This simple exercise will reveal to those running a business why they feel so stressed and why there is never enough time to actually grow the business.

Of course, there will always be the need for you and your key team to do some red and (probably more often) blue activities. The percentage of time spent on each will depend on where the business is in the Stages lifecycle (Chapter 2). But the simple fact is most of us spend too much time stuck in the content of red and blue and far too little in black. This is too much time spent on the P and not enough on the M. However great we are at these admin and revenue-generating activities (after all we've been doing this since the business was started) it really isn't where those who own and run the business add the most value.

How are people spending their time?

The next stage is to look at the next tier down, and the one after that. What are your people really doing? Then create an organisational structure and clear workflows in red, blue and black that suit your business at its current stage of development by assessing which job functions and activities are really needed, allocating roles to the people who are most appropriately skilled or experienced for that job, and then empowering staff to take the responsibilities attached to each role.

It is vital to understand that with each role comes responsibility and it will be necessary to rewrite every job description so that everyone knows their area of activity and the responsibility they will have to solve problems that arise in that area.

The trick is to get each staff member to take real responsibility and for the owners and directors to genuinely delegate and trust staff to fulfil their responsibilities. Allied to a strong culture and a clear vision, this process creates enormous pride and exceptional performance among staff. This in turn creates a hugely productive business where every job is only done once instead of the traditional inefficient system of reporting lines and double-checking every task.

To quote Ajaz Ahmed, Alchemist and founder of AKQA:

> "One of the reasons why it's a struggle for an established organisation to innovate is because the existing team already has its hands full doing the current job."

The key to your asset growth journey is in finding the time to do things differently. To find the time to innovate up that asset ladder. If you are to have any chance of doing this it is essential to create the functional platform that frees you and your senior team from *the current job*.

Benefits of the exercise

Of course, putting in place an efficient functionality structure can take some time and is challenging to achieve without outside help. There will be false starts along the way, but it can have considerable benefits for a business. By doing this exercise properly you should expect to see an increase in productivity of around 30% and that has a massive impact on your bottom line.

More importantly, this exercise creates a large part of the platform you need for future asset growth. Getting this right will help in developing a *culture* where employees feel fully valued and fulfilled and therefore motivated to excel – which we will explore in the next chapter.

An example of this in action is a wonderful company called Roselle Events. Based in Edinburgh, Roselle plans, produces and manages conferences and incentive and recognition events within the corporate sector. After the business was established and for the first few years the founders managed to grow organically.

However, over time, the business started to feel as though it was getting stuck and was not growing as quickly as it had done. CEO and Founder Jo Daley recalls feeling that she didn't have control of the business. She decided to address this by systemising the people side of her business on the principles of red, blue and black to create consistent processes and efficiency in the business. That project took six months to complete but had a huge impact on the culture of the business. Jo says:

> "People began taking responsibility. It's amazing because I couldn't imagine the business without the functional process and structure it has now. Every process is documented too, we have policies and procedures, structure charts and everyone knows what area of the business and which process they are responsible for. So it's a bit like having a logbook for a car with all its service history. Our processes are documented so that it actually becomes an asset in our business which increases the value of it."

Frank Bastow had a similar experience in his own business, but took the idea even further:

> "Now I just don't do red. And I do as little blue as possible. I get other people to do blue. But that's black, isn't it? Getting other people to do red or blue is black! It's really turning those people into assets not costs.
>
> "And I run this at home as well. Me and my wife were saying we know what red, blue and black is at home. Stuff like ironing

and cleaning, they're red, so we sub them out, we give them to someone else. You can turn cooking into a blue because if everyone is getting together and helping out and you then have a meal, then that becomes a blue activity.

"Planning for having fun is a black activity. Planning for the future of your kids – that's a black activity. So if you concentrate on doing black in your business and your personal life, you'll find out that you'll create so much space that you can create more and more black time to do something else, something bigger, create some new assets – whether that's a new business or more time with the family."

"A very good question to ask as you develop your business goal setting strategy . . . do you have the capacity and capability to realise the future?"

Peter Drucker

Capacity

So much for creating a functional business system (and possibly home life). How else can you look to systemise your business as a source activity for building a robust platform for the future and increase operational efficiency?

The answer lies in proper capacity planning.

When I talk to business owners, they can all tell me their turnover and profit margin. But few business owners can tell me the maximum capacity within the business and their current running rate (that is, what percentage of that capacity is being used efficiently).

A business that is making efficient use of all its resources (people, equipment, machinery, etc.) is running at around 80% capacity – there will always be holidays, sickness, plant malfunctions and so on, which will prevent 100% use of resources. Most businesses I meet are operating well below their maximum capacity and consequently are carrying significant extra cost – or put another way, missing significant potential profit.

It is easy to spot businesses with a capacity issue. They are the ones where everyone feels like they are on a treadmill with no way out; people feel busy but the business is not profitable and there's no time to take on more work or plan for the future.

So how do you measure capacity?

If you run an organisation that sells time-based services then you can obviously look at the potential hours available and actual hours sold and see what additional capacity exists within the business. For other types of companies, choose a measure that is appropriate to your business – and you may need a different metric for different functions in the business.

It's then vital to look at what constraints there are in the business. For example, you may have a machine that is *producing* 100 units a day, but if you are only able to *distribute* 50 units a day because of the *functional* efficiency of this part of the business then a bottleneck is in place that constrains your ability to maximise efficiency.

By understanding capacity issues you not only reduce costs but can gain more clarity around business planning and growth strategies. A business that is only working at 50% efficiency (but is unaware of the fact) may feel busy and stretched. When it wants to grow it will probably take on more staff as the CEO is asked to recruit by division heads who are apparently unable to take on any new business. Yet increasing the number of people you employ who are not working efficiently (or to their full capacity) only decreases the company's profitability. It is not growing the business but merely *expanding* it.

Profitable growth occurs when an organisation plans its future in a series of *platform* and *growth* strategies. In a platform phase, the company increases its efficiency and profitability. Platform initiatives may include anything that raises efficiency levels but does not actually grow the capacity of the business. This may be through introducing new systems, through training, or may be achieved by implementing the *efficient functionality* we covered above, since inefficiencies occur when roles overlap and, for example, operational people are spending too much time on administrative tasks.

Returning to the example of the business at 50% capacity, its strategic priority should obviously be on *platform* to fill up that ineffectively used capacity through productivity strategies. Only when the implementation of these platforms has increased the running rate (over time) from 50% to perhaps 75% does the business need to change from a platform to a *growth* strategy to grow the capacity of the business. This growth strategy could involve investing in assets such as additional talent or new premises, acquiring another business, or could be about looking at market position, product channels or pricing strategies.

If the distinction between *platform* and *growth* is confusing imagine a cup half empty (50% capacity). When it is almost full (having followed a platform strategy), the contents need to be tipped into a *bigger* cup – and that is a growth strategy – at which point the contents revert to taking up perhaps 50% of the larger available volume. When you have consolidated that growth (platform strategy again) you will change to another growth strategy. And so on.

The diagram below illustrates this process.

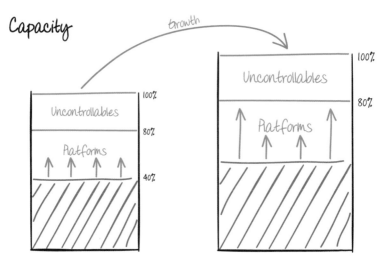

This concept can be used to plan the journey (vision) you would like to take to your commercial goal. For example, you can imagine that a strategy of building your running rate (platform) to 80% before making modest investments to grow your capacity (growth) such that your running rate drops to 65% would feel very different to, say, a more aggressive strategy where the business builds run rate to only 60% before dropping back to 40% through initiatives to dramatically grow capacity before building back to 60% again and then making a further investment in capacity at which point the run rate slips back to 40%.

You can also plan ahead exactly what platform and growth strategies you will adopt and when these will be phased in, how much each will cost, and exactly what impact that will have on your running rate and therefore your profitability. When you get this written down, it will be a far more useful document than most business plans. It will allow you to feel absolutely in control and make a fairly compelling case to your bank.

Understanding this capacity model enables you to plan and develop a profitable growth strategy for your business – and gets you off that treadmill. This can be transformational. You may recall Roger Philby's epiphany from Chapter 2:

> "And then one day I was shown the Shirlaws capacity model. And I kind of went, 'Wow, now I understand the difference between growth and platform. The reason that I've never grown is all I've ever done is growth strategy.' And then I was shown Shirlaws model for functionality. Oh my god! If I put functionality with capacity!"

The first step, however, is to really understand your capacity and run rate numbers. If you have read *Good to Great* by Jim Collins you will recall a central element of his thesis was that businesses that become great fundamentally understand their *business drivers* and that should include your capacity numbers.

You will observe that what I am calling *platform strategies* are often the things you do to get you to benchmark – in other words to build a strong business platform. *Growth strategies*, on the other hand, are all about developing new assets to build a powerful, high-value business. This book is not really concerned with platform strategies other than a few we have considered in this chapter. Growth strategies, on the other hand, will take up the remainder of the book.

Revenue management

The second big area of concern in building your asset-based platform after *costs* is to look at *revenue*; how you sell, deliver and service your customers. Once again, our interest is not with the quality of your product, sales ability or servicing. It is with the design of the system that lies behind your product and revenue creation.

From a valuation point of view, the most important thing to consider on the revenue side is future risk. How reliant you are on a single customer, market or channel, for example. If your future revenues are very reliant on a single customer, or possibly sector, this represents a risk and can devalue the business. From a pure *profit* perspective having all your eggs in one basket can be fine in theory at least. From a *multiple* perspective it represents a future risk and so is likely to reduce the multiple you can command. It's good practice, therefore, to achieve a reasonably broad client and channel base.

Uneven or, worse, dropping revenue will also, rather obviously, have an impact on the multiple, quite apart from on the profit side of the equation. There are any number of reasons why sales revenue may be erratic or falling and it is not the purpose of this book to examine these. However, in terms of looking at revenue as a *system* it is worth considering it in a broader context.

I have always found it useful to look at revenue not in isolation but as part of the whole business. There is a tendency, when revenue is not as good as we would like, to focus on the immediate and the obvious – normally to focus on the sales team. I have usually found that the problem lies further up the *revenue chain*.

If you think of your business as a series of interconnected functions you can imagine there is a flow of value or revenue through each. The business system is therefore rather like a river. Any interruption to the flow will have an impact on revenue. However, the blockage may well not be where the problem is showing up but, rather, upstream. You will see what I mean when you consider this diagram of a revenue system.

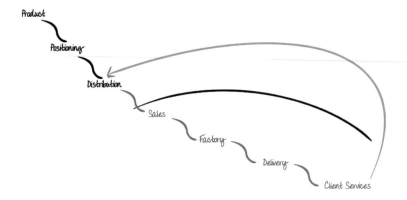

Product
Positioning
Distribution
Sales
Factory
Delivery
Client Services

Management often focus a lot of time on the product and how it is sold and delivered. That's not a bad thing, but it may serve to look at revenue in a broader context, particularly if revenues are under pressure. In the revenue stream diagram I think of product as being in the blue area. The factory is where it is created, the sales step is how the client is engaged, and the delivery is how the client experiences it in reality: "I sell, I make, I deliver."

Real growth of revenue, and the resolution of problems, can often be in none of these areas. For example, very often businesses continue to trade with a proposition that is no longer relevant, or with a market position that has become muddled. It's hard for customers to buy in these circumstances. It's also hard for your distribution channel to effectively serve your proposition to clients.

The thing about revenue in a business is that it tends to be fairly specific to a particular industry or even business type. It's therefore quite hard to give general advice. Some things are, of course, common to all businesses. You have a *product*, a *position* and you have *customers*.

What your business is famous for

What is striking to me about talking to the Alchemists is that they all have an instinctive understanding that what their business is famous for, what it believes in, its position, is the key driver of its sustainable revenue success. They consequently share an almost obsessive focus on the quality and consistency of their product and how that is experienced by the customer. Whether that is Rupert – "People ask what my USP is but I really don't have one other than to do it better than anyone else in the market" – or Keith – "It's just unbelievable attention to detail."

I don't think really successful entrepreneurs get involved in the operational everyday activities of the business. But they do all keep a fundamental focus on the experience the customer has of the product and what the marketplace is saying about it, whether that is Richard Branson walking around the aircraft on every flight he takes or Keith Abel having a veg box delivered every week.

Keith says:

> "When I went back to Abel & Cole when the business was failing I asked a team of about 30 managers how many were getting a delivery from Abel & Cole and the answer was about three or four. And it was perfectly reasonable... the rest were saying 'If I want some stuff I just walk through the warehouse and pick it out,' and you think, 'Well, you're not getting the experience.' It would be like running a restaurant and never eating in it, and just saying 'I go back to the kitchen and I just pick at things.' Well, then you're not going to know that the soup's got hair in it."

Ajaz Ahmed, in his great book *Velocity*, quotes the 29-year-old Steve Jobs:

"When you are a carpenter making a beautiful chest of drawers, you are not going to use a piece of plywood on the back, even though it faces the wall and nobody will ever see it. You'll know it's there."

Ajaz goes on to say:

"If you lose sleep over things 99% of your customers will never notice, you'll spot problems before even your harshest critic has time to do so."

In other words, these entrepreneurs are never fully satisfied and are constantly finessing and improving *what* they do. They have a laser-clear understanding of their position in the market, they constantly build it through what they make, who they employ, how they act, and they constantly find innovative ways to tell people about it.

Keith Abel describes it like this:

"The number one thing is you've got to have people talking about you so we were doing lots of incredibly original things and there were hundreds of them: we were running our vans on bio-diesel; we were washing our vans with caught rain water; we were route-optimising to reduce mileage; we were paying farmers in advance so that they could plant trees; we were agreeing crop prices a year in advance and then sticking to them; we were paying our farmers at 21 days instead of 95 days which is what the supermarkets were doing; we gave up air freighting; we had an ethical audit done in 2001. We had this school scheme where mums from the PTA could sell bags of veg through their school and keep all the profit for themselves – it's now raised over a million quid for primary schools in South London. We recycled our boxes, we used biodegradable plastics to package things.

"It was just absolutely endless that every single area that you looked at we were doing something really groundbreaking and we were telling people exactly which carrot field their carrots came from and giving people competitions to go down and stay on the carrot farm. And every week you'd get a newsletter which was quirky and different and telling the story of some mad nut farmer who had grown something for you and some quirky thing that we'd done.

"So you've got a very cool company, very cool drivers, great story to tell, we're a very quirky bunch, you know? We didn't employ South London white van men, we employed Todd with dreadlocks down to the back of his knees who looked like a model. Friday night he would always go out to a party with customers. And there were lots of drivers who were like that. It had a real personality to it. And very much the culture we built was that people were allowed to just be themselves. We never had scripts for answering the phone. People would just answer it as they want to answer it and because we were interested in employing nice people and that was the key criteria – did we like the person – customers really felt it."

Your customers do your marketing for you

My other key learning is that the Alchemists all understand that the customer is their first channel to market. Ajaz Ahmed puts it like this:

"The thing is that if you make your customers really happy, they ask you to do more. They become your source of new business. For that to happen, we have to share values with our clients. We feel we are in partnership with them. It's a spirit of collaboration. If you are there to be the best you can possibly be and to create the future with clients it's obvious you need to collaborate with them."

Keith Abel shares the sentiment in a business-to-consumer space:

"Firstly, I was personally speaking to customers every day. I'd answer the phone in the afternoon for a couple of hours when we were busy and I'd say, 'What did you think of last week?' etc. And we always phoned people up and said 'Thanks for recommending a friend, look, we'd really like to give you a present, would you like a bottle of wine or would you like a bottle of olive oil?'

"So at every single stage any interaction you had with the company was just a bit different. So everyone's talking about it. So you snowball. When you've got 2000 customers they're only capable of talking to 2000 friends. When you've got 20,000 people talking to you, they're talking to 20,000 friends and when you're a bit more organised all 20,000 are regularly getting marketing materials and 2000 of them respond and it's literally like that. Provided then that after that you're good at what you do and constantly getting better rather than getting worse as you get bigger (which is what a lot of companies do), you know, off you go."

Nick Jenkins also provides his take on this:

"For the first five years, although we lost money, we were constantly growing. We couldn't find a cost-effective form of customer acquisition but through all of that was that, without doing any marketing at all, our sales were growing 30-40% a year. That was because customers were begetting customers and that taught me one of the very early lessons; if you get the product or the service right then your customers will do your marketing for you. And by doing a bit more marketing, that's just oiling the wheels really. I really think people love to recommend – they want the glory of passing on a good idea. People do it all the time, they recommend restaurants, they recommend holiday companies.

"A personal recommendation is at its best when it is unsolicited. A lot of people suggest that we should do 'recommend a friend' but generally the reward doesn't make any difference and you make a serious dent in your gross margin. Your customers are not doing it for financial reward. You should just rely on the fact that, if you get it right, your customer will want their friends to do it because they think it's a good thing for them to do."

Reviewing your process

So, if your revenue numbers are not as good as you would wish them to be there are a number of other things you should review before taking the right professional advice (whether that advice is in sales, marketing or strategy).

Take a look at the revenue stream diagram. Score your business honestly in each area against what you feel you *should* be achieving. You can do this with scores out of ten or with a tick/neutral/cross. Either way you should get a good sense of where the blockages are.

Then interrogate each area in turn:

a. Is your core product proposition your absolute focus? Is it still relevant and attractive? Are you always good at what you do and getting better not worse, etc.? This is the essential foundation of your business – are you personally experiencing it? Are you talking to customers all the time personally? If you are still doing a good job and yet revenues are declining, has something fundamental happened in that product area that you have not adapted to? Has the world moved on? Are you still selling a boom product in a bust market? As the economy recovers and customers look for new ideas are you still relevant?

b. If so, is the way you position and communicate yourself as sharp as it could be? Who are you (as a business)? What are you famous for? Do you know how customers, prospects and competitors would answer that question? (If not ask them.) Are all your messages consistent with that in the way Keith Abel described above? If your position has become fuzzy or muddled it's hard to be heard.

c. If you have a pin-sharp *position* are you leveraging that really effectively in your distribution channel? We have talked about using customers as a channel, but how else will your prospective customers gain easy access to your product? What is the supermarket to your Heinz? You may feel that you don't have a distribution channel other than advertising or sales. But I would challenge you to think deeply about who your customers trust for advice and work out strategies to educate and develop that channel. It might be the internet if you are selling products. But it might be other professional advisors if you are selling services. Having a channel that constantly refers your product to the ideal customer is the single most powerful system you can build on your revenue (blue) side. To learn more about this you might have a read of my short book *More Money, More Time, Less Stress*. Take a look at www.shirlawscoaching.co.uk where you can download a free copy.

In other words, it's vitally important to critically assess your product and how it is delivered within an entire revenue system. Is your core proposition relevant? Is your position clear and distinct and will it create cut-through in your marketplace? Are you using that position to power a distribution strategy? Then you can look at how well you sell and meet your promise to your customers.

Finally, take a serious look at how you service your customers. What clear strategy do you have in place to service customers after, by which I mean *between*, sales? Rupert Lee-Browne of Caxton tells a powerful story to illustrate this absolute focus on service. It made me think about whether I *really* understand customer service and is well worth repeating:

> "We had a good client called Ray who was buying a plot of land next to his house in France. He was a very organised guy: he organised his transfer of money to us, we did the exchange for him. He gave us perfect details and we sent out the money to the right account at the French Post Office. Who then promptly lost his money. The closer we got to completion the more irate he got, as you might anticipate, and the Thursday before he completed on the Friday we discovered where the money was. It was coming back to us, which was useless. So I phoned him up and I said, 'Ray, I will meet you at Carcassonne Airport tomorrow morning with the money.' I then booked a Ryanair flight; I got on the plane with a bankers draft in my pocket and delivered it to him in person. The guy was blown over. He said no bank in the world would ever do this for me, to have the Chief Executive fly out with the money. It was a tiny amount, EUR8,500, but I wasn't prepared to lose the reputation of the business on it."

Other than to immediately open an account with Caxton FX, which I did and would heartily recommend, what I took from this was that if you truly believe in service, and if that is the context against which you run your business, it is not equivocal. It is absolute. For more great stories of exceptional customer service I recommend Tony Hsieh's book, *Delivering Happiness*.

To quote Harvey MacKay: "There's a place in the world for any business that takes care of its customers – after the sale." This is a strategic function and any good business will have a clear system to service customers and drive sustainable loyalty. I talk more about this in *More Money, More Time, Less Stress*.

That's all I want to say about revenue in terms of creating the right *platform*. We will examine product in asset terms in far greater depth in later chapters.

Assets and liability management

Now we turn to the balance sheet.

To quote the brilliant David Molian of Cranfield School of Management, one of the most highly regarded centres of excellence for entrepreneurship:

> "A strong balance sheet is the best security for the future, so seize every opportunity to shore it up."

What does that mean, exactly?

From a valuation perspective assets and liabilities are the next thing a valuer or buyer will look for after the P&L. Having surprises here is even more damaging than having your costs and revenues out of kilter because it can be more detrimental to the long-term value of the business. It also tends to indicate other operational or management issues. At best, it is a distraction.

This is an area where you are best to seek the advice of an experienced accountant to take a detailed look at all your tangible assets and any liabilities. Getting them cleaned up now has an immediate impact on your asset value, but more importantly allows you to build the intangible assets which are the real focus of this book.

From an assets perspective, here is the checklist that Guy Rigby helpfully provides in *From Vision to Exit*:

- Control and protect your assets

- Ensure your assets are under your ownership or otherwise contractually protected

- Make sure you accurately record your assets

- Check your assets are insured

- Exploit your assets efficiently

- Don't invest in tangible assets unless you can be sure of a return well above your cost of capital

- Consider leasing assets to reduce capital costs

Guy also makes helpful reference to intangible assets, which we will cover in later chapters:

- Managing intangible assets

- Make sure any vital intellectual property is under your ownership, registered for patent or trademark if possible, or properly protected by licence agreements

- Keep assets under review – review licence agreements and keep an eye out for use of your IP without permission

- Manage your talent

- Systemise your customer relationship and delivery quality

Your management team

So far in this chapter I have talked about cost (and specifically *strategic resources*), revenue (and specifically *product* and *channel*) and touched on assets and liabilities. The next critical element you need to get right in your platform is obviously your management team and your management system.

I say *obviously* because if you ask any VC or PE house what they mainly look for in a business, the quality of the management team is always high on the list. Having a deficient team is a very effective way to depress the value of your business. In fact, poor management is more damaging to your wealth than anything on the P&L and balance sheet we have covered above. Without the right management you can't grow your assets; It will require too much of your time to build your pyramid.

To quote David Molian of Cranfield School of Management again:

> "Unless you can recruit, retain and motivate talented people you will never buy yourself the time to free yourself from doing the operational stuff that has to come first. Successful recruitment will allow the owner manager to spend a significant amount of time in creating and fashioning the business of tomorrow."

Critical here is to link the quality of your management team to your vision. The question to ask is not "Do I have the team I need now?" but rather "Do I have the team to get me to where I want to be, the team for my asset journey?"

Russell Stinson recognises finding the right people for the right job and the succession of responsibility from the top team as soon as possible as key to ACT Clean's ability to grow:

> "I've seen people before who think they've got all the answers and it was clear that they were missing a lot of opportunity to develop themselves and to develop the business. And I think we've been self-aware enough to recognise that actually there's

people with skills that can help us and that actually there are probably people in certain areas of the business, whether it's finance, HR, operations, business development, who are probably better than us."

What Russell is saying is that very often a business outgrows its management. It's critical for you to recognise gaps in your core team. It's equally important for you to recognise the strengths and weaknesses in your own capability. Eventually you should hope that your management team outgrows you; building a team that is better than you are is not just a cliché. Whilst doing this, you also need to constantly up your own skills both to keep you fresh and engaged and to drive the business asset journey.

Keith Abel's story is typical:

"And then I got in a really brilliant woman called Ella. Her dad came to help me out and he taught me about business culture, about management which I'd never really been taught before. He made me read books like Stephen Covey's *7 Habits*. And then Ella came along and she was absolutely brilliant at management and I realised straightaway that I was just absolutely crap at management, and really shouldn't be doing it.

"We had a really helpful day, we realised that going away for the day and thinking about things strategically with our top ten people was a really good idea. And good fun. It started off being just Ella and I, then we got more people involved and in one of the exercises we examined Belbin. Are you familiar with Belbin? [Keith is referring to Belbin's Team Roles Model that identifies people's behavioural strengths and weaknesses in their business, www.belbin.com.] I'd never heard of Belbin and I just thought I was being thick and that Ella was really clever, and everyone else seemed to be much better at business than me, but I was greatly encouraged to find that I had a very unique attribute in that I was the ideas guy.

"So then I was able to concentrate on what I was good at and they would focus on making sure that they implemented it. They were very disciplined, they made me very disciplined over how many new ideas I could come up and what the right forum for them was. I didn't really understand the concept of the chain of command so I'd kind of go up and have a really enthusiastic conversation with someone in customer services but that person was in the middle of implementing some new services for customer services and then they'd think, why is the boss telling me to do this? So we just got the chain of command stuff worked out."

Skills gaps, wherever they lie, need to be addressed urgently. This might be through employing new people or re-tasking (through a functionality exercise), or through education of the existing team (Cranfield has an impressive series of entrepreneurial and executive programmes).

It could also be through engaging stronger advisors (e.g. upgrading your accountant), or engaging support within the business either through investing in business coaching, or putting a NED (non-executive director) on your board.

Ultimately, though, sometimes individuals are simply not up to scratch and you need to face that without sentiment.

> *"One of the biggest things I see is companies that start with the team that can't get it to the next level."*

Julie Mayer, Ariadne Capital

When looking at your team it's important to try and be objective. Do you have the right skills across the business disciplines and for the next phase of your growth? Look for capability gaps and find ways to fill them either through training, engaging outside suppliers or hiring new talent.

Don't underestimate the challenges of bringing in new people to an established team. If you can upskill your existing people all the better, but don't let sentiment cloud your judgement. Be honest with your team about how expectations will be set, how the future will be charted and what their place in that future is to be.

We will look at talent and capabilities in much more depth in Chapter 6.

The management team:
The Alchemist's view

In conversation with Russell Stinson

Russell, how about your management team? That's where most businesses feel they have a hole in their asset value. They don't necessarily have the management to get them to the next level. It feels to me like you focus a lot on developing your senior team and the next layer and the next layer after that.

"I think we realised probably about three years ago that as four individuals we couldn't sustain the growth long term. We have developed at operations manager level, supervisor manager level, but we realised that in order to have the scalability we had to bring in quality individuals who could continue their development.

"I think it was about two and a half years ago we brought in a finance director, HR director, operations director, head of training and a quality monitoring manager. We tried to bring in quality people who really know the industry but there's been a real focus on the training and development of people who are within their team. So everything that we do from a coaching point of view and from a development point of view is developing the team."

You're quite conscious of building a management team to get you to your vision rather than reacting to circumstances?

"For me, without it we would get nowhere near it. It's a people business. Everything that we do is people-orientated and there's a real focus on ensuring that our people have got the skills they need for their roles now and for the future as we grow. We have external business coaching and we invest heavily in training at all levels. We are not doing this just with the four of us, there's a management development programme with 20 members of our team because we understand that it's essential that people who are in key roles within the business have got the skill set to help them develop themselves but also to help them develop the team that they run."

Two and a half years ago you upgraded. You brought in a lot of new director-level people. What was the trigger for that? Was there anything specific? Did you have a retreat or something?

"We did... we were away for a couple of days and part of it was to discuss giving us the capacity to grow because we couldn't do it in our current state. I wasn't having the time to spend on the strategic development of the business that I needed to because I was getting dragged into day-to-day issues. It was clear that I needed someone to come in to take that away.

"It was exactly the same for Paul, to give him the opportunity to coach, develop, to spend time with clients, to support John's business development side. From the HR point of view Rob needed someone to come in and take the day-to-day issues away from him. So it was really that reality check, that you know what, for us to double the next year we needed to have quality people come in to help us with all the day to day."

Do you see them as an asset in financial terms? Or is it that we need a management team to enable us to drive more revenue?

"For me, our company is about people so every single member of our team is a key asset. The scalability, the delivery of the service, everything around that depends on our people."

External risk

The last layer below the benchmark line, and the one most damaging to the future value of your business, contains the external risks to your business: economic, political and technological. Self-evidently, this is the layer most outside of your control.

The key watchword here is *awareness*. Running a business, it is critical to be constantly aware of what is going on both in your sector and in the wider world. It is your job to be constantly asking the "What if...?" questions. You need to be asking what impact political, macroeconomic or disruptive technological shifts could have on the business in two, three or five years' time and adapt and innovate accordingly. We will look at this habit in more detail in Chapter 7.

When I hadn't a clue and ran my businesses in a wholly P&L-focussed operational way, rather than seeing the business from an asset perspective, one of the consequences was that I felt very much at the mercy of things outside of my control. But I have come to realise that, whilst we have no control over external factors, we certainly can respond and adapt to them if we can develop the right mindset. In my conversations with the Alchemists this mindset is a clear factor contributing to their success.

I think an understanding of your core assets is the key to this, as I hope will become clear throughout the book. We'll look in Chapter 7 at the Wenham Lake Ice Company as a classic example of a great business destroyed by external factors. Whilst the management had no control over these factors, they could have responded to and even harnessed them to their advantage. The business could still be around to this day if they had done so.

The example of the *external factor* that comes most to mind right now, of course, is the global economy and the impact on almost all of us of the 2007 to 2012 *Depression*. This external factor destroyed a lot of good businesses but I would argue that those businesses most in tune with their assets not only survived but thrived in this period. By focussing on their real assets and not just the P&L, they were more able to adapt. The Abel & Cole story of the impact of the recession on an overly P&L-focussed management team and the asset-based recovery plan that grew the business to £50m whilst in a recession (see Chapter 2) is a great example of this.

Not that profit is unimportant. As I have said before, it is vital and this is why the chapter began by looking at this subject. It is just that an exclusive focus on that side of the equation can make the business blind to wider threats and opportunities. My own experience of the recent recession from the perspective of the valuation layers may be instructive. I have certainly learnt more in the last four years than in the whole of the rest of my career. And, like Aconcagua, it hasn't all been fun.

My experience of the valuation layers

I took over as CEO of Shirlaws at the end of 2008. The previous management team had done a remarkable job in holding everything together as the market fell off a cliff. It was an extraordinary time to be in business; I recall in 2007 hearing the chief economist of HSBC say that there was no structural reason why the UK should follow the US into recession but "we could have one if we wanted one."

Clearly we all decided that is exactly what we wanted and we all panicked at the same time. Consequently, despite doing a fine job, the pace of recession was such that our management team had inevitably not reacted fast enough and we had not unwound far enough. My task was therefore fairly obvious, but it is interesting in relation to the discussions about getting to benchmark in this chapter.

My first job was cost management – damage control on the P&L. Expensive people who left were not replaced, we downsized offices, etc. I remember talking a lot about the Rutherford Principle – "we haven't any money so we'll just have to *think*" – at this point. It's a useful mantra.

I found great benefit in creative ways of working with suppliers – in informal skill exchange, for example. We also had to do a lot quite quickly so introduced the *10 things in 100 days*, which I'll talk about in Chapter 5. The point was to get our cost base *well below comfortable breakeven* to start to rebuild cash. In my experience businesses rarely get costs low enough fast enough and consequently run out of cash (see Guy Rigby's insights above).

With costs under comfortable control the next *10 things* were to look at revenue management, the other half of the P&L. I was conscious at the time that I was acting as a very operational, P&L-focussed

CEO (and I recall the detailed level of scrutiny from the board!). But it was required in the circumstances.

The consequence of all of this activity was an improved balance sheet with dramatically reduced liabilities (debt) and improved assets (in our case mainly cash). What made this process relatively easy was that whilst external factors had moved against us, fundamentally we had a good business with a strong culture, exceptional talent and a great product. It was clear to us that we were simply not leveraging these intangible assets as effectively as we might.

I remember a strategic retreat to the wonderful Spread Eagle Hotel in Sussex at which we chose to change how we ran the business, from a revenue to an asset perspective, into the economic recovery that was still two years away but we knew would come.

In order to do this we had the business professionally valued by our sister company Assay Advisory (www.assaycf.com). It was a revelatory experience for an executive team and one I would recommend. We took this step not with any idea of selling it but as a means to better manage business growth. It was just as Russell Stinson articulated in an earlier chapter:

> "Measuring the value of our business is about driving our strategic direction. We see our business as an asset."

And what did the valuation reveal?

We scored well on the P&L and balance sheet that had been our recent focus but, to some amusement from the board, the gap in our valuation layers occurred at *management quality*. Me. What the report made clear was that whilst we had some fantastic intangible assets that had the potential to create a significant uplift in valuation (culture, talent, product etc.), these could not be fully leveraged with the executive focussed, as we still were, *inward* and not *outward*, and on revenue and not assets.

It taught me to change the way I ran the business. My *10 things* became centred on moving my focus as CEO literally 100% out of red and progressively out of blue. My future was wholly in black. To allow for this we invested in the leadership team, bringing in expertise in marketing and in product. Most dramatically we appointed a managing director to completely run the operations of the business whilst I focused entirely on growth and entirely on the asset journey.

Top tips for building a winning business platform

To complete my raid on *From Vision to Exit*, here is a summary of the top tips provided by Guy Rigby, liberally sprinkled with my own additions. Some of this is *business 101* but it is an excellent checklist. If you feel your business has not fully systemised in any area I would urge you to get hold of a copy of Guy's book or talk to your accountant.

- Make sure that you or someone you trust is keeping the financial score in your business. **Don't penny pinch on the management of your financial position**.

- **Keep proper books of account**, electronically or otherwise, so that accurate financial data can be extracted easily and efficiently.

- **Prepare integrated budgets and forecasts** to predict your expectations for the business. Challenge your assumptions and beware of errors or omissions.

- **Prepare monthly management accounts** and review these against your budgets and forecasts. Investigate variances and consider whether corrective action is required.

- **Implement daily or weekly reporting** to keep management abreast of key financial developments and KPIs. Use this information as a management tool to help you run your business.

- **Monitor the key financial ratios** in your business and investigate any unexpected changes.

- **Keep direct and indirect costs under review at all times**. Actively manage the balance between fixed and variable costs in your business to maintain flexibility. Don't forget hidden costs such as staff inefficiencies or difficult customer relationships.

- **Structuring and resourcing must be a strategic function** and not one that is dictated from the bottom up.

- If you want **real productivity** you can't give people responsibility, they have to take it for themselves, so create a system and culture that allows for this.

- **Choose your customers carefully and keep your debtors under control at all times**. Your debtors deliver the cash that drives your business.

- **Know the capacity of your business** and current running rate – these enable you to plan and develop a profitable growth strategy. Understand where the bottlenecks that choke the profitability of your business are – and release them.

- Understand the **difference between platform strategies and growth strategies** and use these to maximise profitability today and plan your growth tomorrow.

- **Select an appropriate bank** for your business and focus on building a strong and trusting relationship in both good times and bad. Always say what you will do and do what you say.

- Regularly ask yourself if you **have the right team to reach your asset goal**. Recognise gaps in your own capability and those in your core team. Be honest with yourself and with them.

- **Prioritise areas for investment in your business.** Make investments that will increase the capability or profitability of the business, helping you towards the attainment of your vision.

- **Control and protect your assets** and, where possible, build reserves to strengthen your balance sheet. Don't forget the importance of your intangible assets.

- **Examine your revenue performance** as part of the whole business system and don't just focus on sales. Look *upstream*. Develop a broad customer base and avoid revenue concentration on one or two customers.

- **Make sure you can articulate specifically what it is you are famous for**. Do you have a laser focus?

- **Your customers are your primary channel**. Talk to them. Constantly focus on their experience. Make certain that you are good at what you do and constantly getting better rather than getting worse.

- **Service your customers between sales**. If you truly believe in service it is not equivocal, it is absolute.

- **Ensure you have the right team in place**. Poor management is usually more damaging to your wealth than anything on the P&L and balance sheet. Make sure you have the team in place for your asset journey and not just for where you are today. Seek outside help to address skills gaps.

- As CEO **it is critical to stay constantly aware of what is going on in the wider world** and what opportunities and threats that presents.

Action plan: Ten things to do now

1. Have a complete review of your platform and **make sure you are getting the fundamentals right**. Monitoring and measurement is critical so that you can move on.

2. **Review your diary for this month**. Systematically colour-code each meeting, appointment or task in red, blue and black. What percentage of your time do you spend in each colour? Begin a functionality project – create an organisational structure and workflow in red, blue and black for the business that spreads responsibility better and frees you and your senior team from the current job to create time for you to innovate up that asset ladder.

3. **Hold a strategic retreat this quarter** devoted to the platform. Examine all the elements below benchmark with your senior team and work out how you can better systemise and monitor these and who will be responsible for each.

4. Start to **develop a capacity plan** which you can use as a daily management tool and a key monthly measurement of performance.

5. **Examine your position and product**. Are you absolutely clear of your position in the market? Can you articulate exactly what you are best in the world at and is everyone in the organisation, everything they do and everything you say consistent with this? Is your product absolutely the best it can be?

6. Make a commitment to **truly understand your customers' experience**. Use your product, website, etc. Talk to your customers directly. Ask your people how they think you can improve.

7. **Put together a servicing strategy for your customers**. Think creatively about how you can delight them between sales. Involve them in the business as much as possible.

8. **Focus on your management team**. Continue to upskill yourself and your team. Ask them what further learning they would value. Consider having some education together as a team. Review your functionality and capacity plans to identify any developing skills gaps. Look at least two years ahead; do you have the team to get you to where you want to be? Hire early.

9. **Look outside of your business**. Make the time to read widely. Attend business talks and thought-leading events. Don't get stuck in today.

10. **Get valued**. Seriously consider having your business formally valued and invest in a report that shows you specifically what you need to do to drive your asset strategy. We used Assay Advisory (www.assaycf.com) and it changed how we ran the business.

Chapter 4.
Sunscreen for Scaffolders

"Business must be run at a profit, else it will die, but when anyone tries to run a business solely for profit ... then also the business must die, for it no longer has a reason for existence."

Henry Ford

Building the performance culture

V+7	Scale
V+6	Brand architecture
V+5	Channel extension
V+4	Product extension
V+3	Systems / product innovation
(V+2)	Talent / capability / culture
VI	——————————————— Industry benchmark

HAVING SET OUT TO WRITE A BOOK ABOUT BUILDING POWERFUL long-term assets I have just subjected you to a whole chapter on short-term profit. I apologise but it needed to be covered in the context of ensuring a platform for the sustainable asset-based business. Of course, profit is vitally important for the business. It's just that it's not, in my view, the overriding focus of the CEO of a growth business.

As Peter Drucker says, "Profit should be the mere consequence and not the main goal of a business." In other words, profit flows as a consequence of getting other things right. And, once your robust platform is in place, those things are your assets. After all, ask any investment professional and they'll tell you "income follows asset."

In the introduction you may recall I said that I had been on something of a quest to find out what really drives this sustainable value and what underpins the most successful private businesses. I said that I now understand the alchemy that creates this fundamental value.

What I have learnt is that it all starts with one word: *why*.

Aligned, motivated and committed people

I have the good fortune to meet hundreds of entrepreneurs a year and find out what makes their businesses tick. All the most successful businesses I see, those with real potential scale and longevity, those I most admire, have one thing in common. That is a clearly defined, aligned and powerful culture. Great business starts with great culture.

At the core of *Good to Great*, Jim Collins has three key principles:

1. understand what you can be *best in the world* at

2. understand your key *economic drivers*

3. understand what you *believe* in and are deeply passionate about

In my experience, the most important of these is the last. By galvanising your team behind a common set of beliefs – a common culture – you create the environment in which the other two are possible.

Not that the other two principles are not vital. *What* you are best in the world at is, to me, another way of describing your fundamental value proposition. I call this a business' intellectual property and I will come on to cover this in later chapters.

Also, in a mid-sized private business at least, *how* your key economic drivers power your business engine is largely contained in the platform (benchmark) discussion we looked at in the previous chapter. But in my experience it all starts with *why*.

Great businesses are *why* businesses because their people are aligned behind and engaged in a single, common purpose. That alignment in a shared belief drives excellence, creativity, innovation and sheer hard work. Put another way, people will naturally follow the path of least resistance if not given a compelling reason to do more and to go further.

One of the best business books I've read in recent years is Simon Sinek's *Start with Why*. In it Simon makes the simple statement that:

> "When people believe in what you believe in they'll work with their blood, sweat and tears. When they don't believe in what you believe in they'll work for your money."

It's a cliché that a business' greatest asset is its people. It's half true. A business' greatest asset is its people when they are aligned, motivated and passionately committed to collective success. Otherwise they're a cost.

In other words, business *culture* is an asset because it allows for all the future wealth-generative stuff to happen. Without a great performance culture it's hard to see how a business can build any significant assets. It's hard to see how a business can innovate. On this theme, the late, great Steve Jobs once said:

> "Innovation has nothing to do with how many R&D dollars you have. It's not about money. When Apple came up with the Mac,

IBM was spending at least 100 times more on R&D. It's about the people you have, how they're led, and how much you get it."

Innovation, growth and wealth are sourced in great culture; great culture comes from a shared belief; belief comes from inspiring leadership. And inspiring leadership is, of course, the job of those leading the business. It is our job.

It is our job to set and articulate the *why* for your business. It is our job to inspire and not just to have a great strategy. People are always inspired by *why* more than *what*. To quote Simon Sinek again:

> "Martin Luther King did not stand up in front of a quarter of a million people in Washington Mall in August 1963 and say 'I have a plan.'"

Articulating the dream is your day job. And that starts with articulating why your company exists. A great question to ask yourself and your team is: does your business *deserve* to exist? Would the world be poorer without it?

That should help clarify what purpose your business serves. One of the great joys of a private business is that we can pursue a purpose that is not shackled by narrow shareholder interests. Of course it's possible for a plc too, but is a lot harder.

Putting the ding in your universe

Your most important act as leader is therefore to articulate that purpose. Right back in 1980 Bill Gates set Microsoft's intention to have "a computer on every desk and in every home." Steve Jobs once said Apple's purpose was to put "a ding in the universe" and that drive towards creating radical new solutions based on great design informs everything Apple does. That passionate alignment and belief in a common purpose runs right through Apple, as is evident in how staff appear in any Apple store. It is the Apple culture.

You don't have to be Apple but if you are seriously embarked on this asset journey, it's vital that you take time to discover your own purpose. Now. As Frank Bastow articulated in Chapter 2, "That's what I tell everyone, (it's) really easy if you know what your intent is."

I know a small business with the clear intent or purpose "to create the freedom to be extraordinary." That intent drives everything they do and every key decision they make. It creates a team who care passionately about the company, each other and their customers. They want to create *extraordinary* every day and are given the freedom to do so. We'll come back to freedom in a moment.

Ajaz Ahmed is absolutely clear that:

"Making money has never been our intention and yet, commercially, we outperform our competitors. Right from day one, we have had the clear intention to 'help our clients to create the future.'"

Keith Abel was equally clear what Abel & Cole believed in. This showed up in the staff they attracted, how they behaved and the service the customers received.

"Yes, we had a set of genuinely held beliefs and we were very clear about mapping what those beliefs were. So we've got these charts that say this is what Abel & Cole is all about. There were posters on the wall basically saying 'happy customers, happy employees, happy suppliers, happy environment, and happy community, happy Abel & Cole.' We believe that we better put things back into the community, treat our suppliers fairly, be respectful towards our employees, look after the environment, etc.

"We never really thought about profit. Obviously in the background we were being very careful about margin and cost but that wasn't the big focus of attention. And it was very unauthoritarian. Although possibly it was very carefully, strategically led, you didn't feel like you had some shitty boss telling you what to do."

Profit wasn't the focus of attention

In my own business we have a firmly held belief that our purpose is to "change people's lives." You won't find this statement in our external communication or on our website. It's not about what we tell other people. It is about what we believe in ourselves. It is the common and shared purpose that holds us together as an organisation all over the world and drives our culture. It is the context against which all our choices are made.

Since it is the foundation of our culture it drives who we attract both in terms of our own talent and customers who choose to work with us. It infuses everything we do as an organisation. Given that what we do is fairly commercial (help to build successful businesses) it's amazing how often customers will write to me and use the exact words that working with us has "changed their lives."

So take the time, this year, to uncover and agree the intent in your business. What purpose do you serve? It doesn't have to be altruistic or spiritual but it should be something that you and your team can take pride in. It could be to serve your customers, but try to find some emotive language that will engage your people at a deeper level. Here are some statements of intent that I have come across that I like:

- *To help people live well and die old.* Innocent

- *To provide the best customer service possible.* Zappos

- *To change the way we do business, one entrepreneur at a time.* UnLtd

- *To put a ding in the universe.* Apple

- *To give people the freedom to be extraordinary.* onefish twofish

- *To ride with our customers.* Harley Davidson

- *To be the UK's most trusted energy supplier.* Ovo Energy

- *To create opportunities for everyone to be brilliant at work.* Chemistry Group

- *To create the future with our clients.* AKQA

Take your key team offsite for a couple of days and use the time to find the answer for your business and align yourselves around it. Pay for someone good to facilitate this process. This is the fundamental source of the performance culture you need to build.

The three great motivators

In his masterful book *Drive*, which I would urge you to read, Dan Pink talks about the three great motivators of human organisational performance (and none of them are money). If you want to achieve a true performance culture you need to harness these three drivers.

The first is purpose – the sense that you are working towards a shared and higher goal. The sense that you believe in what your organisation believes in and are not just working for money.

The second is autonomy – the sense that you have the freedom to take independent action and are sufficiently valued and respected to be allowed that freedom. The truth is that most organisations attempt to control their people far more than is necessary – or commercially healthy. This control comes from our fear as owners and managers and is counterproductive to the creation of an innovative culture that builds assets and wealth.

Reed Hastings, the highly successful CEO of Netflix, comments "responsible people thrive on freedom and are worthy of freedom." In other words, once you have clearly articulated the context (the purpose), the most productive course is to get out of the way and give your team the autonomy – the freedom – to deliver. Hastings goes further:

> "If you're the manager and your people fail, don't blame them. Ask yourself how you created a context that allowed them to fail."

This, of course, presupposes your people are sufficiently talented, but we'll explore that in a later chapter.

Freedom is not about anarchy, it is about setting a clear and motivating purpose (a why) that creates the context for your people to operate independently and efficiently. I'll pick up this habit of successful leaders in the next chapter.

What of the third great performance driver revealed by Dan Pink? That is mastery – the desire we all have to learn, to grow, to explore. To be extraordinary. If your culture is not one of learning and openness, if you do not encourage your people to develop personally and professionally – every day – you are simply not getting the most out of them.

So, my strongest advice is to think about your culture. Is it based on the three principles of purpose, autonomy and mastery? Are you crystal clear on why you deserve to exist? Are you inspiring and rallying your people and their passions around that purpose? Are you setting the context? Do you have the courage and confidence to genuinely give your people autonomy? Is yours really a learning culture in which your people grow and develop every day?

If not, now is the time to do something about it. A culture is not expensive to create. It just takes time and commitment. Done well, it can be a massive asset in the business and is the foundation of your whole asset journey. The journey starts with why.

The value of values

Before moving on from culture let's just touch on the topic of values. For too many businesses coming up with some half-remembered values and going out for the occasional pizza is about the extent of their cultural strategy. These are businesses that do not have culture as a leverageable asset. They are not getting any value from their values.

Yet values can be an incredibly important part of practically building a great culture. It is the natural next step from setting your intent. There are three rules. If you ignore these, your values are unlikely to become the building blocks of a great culture:

1. Your values must be shared by the whole team and not imposed.

2. Everyone must understand what these values mean in your business, what behaviours they are judged against, and be able to articulate both.

3. You must live your values and refresh them regularly.

None of this is hard. You just need to make the time to do it.

The problem is that most of us come up with a list of values and then kind of forget about them. Or have them as part of our external communication because we think we should. Often we end up with values that look like this:

- Integrity

- Communication

- Respect

- Excellence

Are these, in your opinion, good values? Well, yes, of course they are if they follow the rules set out above: shared, understood and lived. The four words above are the values of Enron. They were imposed, forgotten and ignored.

So here is what I think you need to do. Unless you have recently conducted a full and proper values exercise that you are proud of, do one this quarter. Appoint a champion to run it, but you MUST be actively involved as sponsor.

Have your champion run a workshop or series of workshops (depending on the size and complexity of the business) so that everyone has the chance to contribute. They will end up with a long list of values. Now they must reduce that to three core values (at most four) which are effectively the higher or context words of a longer sub-list. It's a good idea to have the champion appoint a small team to help with this.

Then the team must define each of those values in a way that is meaningful, powerful and memorable to your organisation. This is a process of communication and involvement with your whole business.

Finally the team must suggest and achieve universal buy-in for a list of specific behaviours that the whole business can measure individual, team and business performance by. These behaviours can be incredibly prosaic but should be specific.

Value – meaning – behaviour

Then publish, use and LIVE the values. Paint them on the wall. Have them inform every aspect of how you recruit, promote, reward, manage, communicate and celebrate in your business. And revisit them twice a year to check in.

If this sounds too hard then I would urge you to get some outside help. It is well worth the investment to get this right. It's fundamental to your asset journey.

One of my favourite stories about facilitating a values exercise involved an august, well-known and historic publishing company. The champion was a wonderful lady of a certain age. One of the values they came up with was passionate. It's a great value if it has meaning but is very often just a blancmange value. On being challenged pretty hard as to what it meant the team clung tenaciously to it. The clincher was when the champion looked over her half-moon glasses and said, "It means, dear, that we give a fuck. We give a fuck for our customers, we give a fuck for our business, and we give a fuck for each other."

And that is the definition that is literally still written down and enshrined in the values document of this illustrious publishing house. It is meaningful, powerful and memorable. It can also be judged using some simple behaviours which are no more complex than "We ALWAYS answer the phone by the third ring," and "We ALWAYS celebrate each other's birthdays," etc.

I mentioned earlier that my business' intent to change people's lives is central to and underpins our culture. When I sat together with my team at the retreat in the Spread Eagle Hotel and looked at the business from an asset perspective, we realised just how powerful an asset this culture potentially was.

Potentially because, as I mentioned in the previous chapter, the way I was running the business prevented us fully from harnessing this cultural asset. It prevented us getting to benchmark. Just like Alchemists Roger and Frank, we recognised that, although a great asset, our culture needed to be nurtured.

One of the central aspects that our culture had originally been built upon was that the whole business went away to a top hotel for three days, three times a year, on a strategic retreat. In the recession we had lost some focus on this and we agreed we would reestablish this commitment. It's a commitment we have stuck to since. The point is simply that, whatever your cultural ingredients are, they need to be constantly nurtured and supported. As the animal welfare charities say about puppies, I say about culture: "Culture is for life and not just for Christmas."

What I observed on that mountain in the Andes was that two things kept us going towards the summit. Firstly the system – the planning, process and platform or organisation. This is all the good stuff we covered in the last chapter. And the second was the culture of the team. We climbed the mountain as a team because we had a shared sense of purpose and a bond formed in adversity. The source of that team spirit was the quiet leadership, clear vision and absolute confidence of one man – our leader. It's leadership I want to turn to in the next chapter.

The Alchemist's view

Before we look at leadership, let's hear from our Alchemists, who have built extraordinary cultures in ordinary businesses. As you read, look out for Dan Pink's *purpose*, *autonomy* and *mastery*. Look out for intent and values.

In conversation with Ajaz Ahmed

Ajaz, AKQA is the largest and most recognised digital agency in the world. What have you learnt on that extraordinary journey?

"For thousands of years the only real career for most people was to be a farmer, so it's in all of our DNA. To be a good farmer you need to do everything that's within your control really well. And if you do that then the aspects that are outside of your control – like the weather – will have less of an adverse effect when it inevitably does not go the ideal way. So, I think business is just like a farm – you reap what you sow and you have to make hay while the sun shines."

What does farming have to teach business? What makes great and not merely good?

"You have to want a great crop. You have to want to deliver the best produce for your customers. You have to respect and care for the livestock. You need wise stewardship of resources and the environment. Get up early, work hard – and keep it organic!"

What is the intent behind AKQA?

"We have an absolute belief in the *virtuous circle*. Making money has never been our intention and yet, commercially, we outperform our competitors. Right from day one, we have had the clear intention to "help our clients to create the future." And from day one we have built the business on shared values of Innovation, Service, Quality and Thought. My job is to champion those values and ensure that we create a culture of excellence where mediocrity is not tolerated and is put out of its misery."

And does that form the context for everything you do?

"Yes, those values underpin everything we do."

How do you feel about AKQA?

"I feel that if I didn't work at AKQA, I would most probably want to work at AKQA! It has a great team of people that really care about the clients, care about the work and care about the company."

Why?

"Because AKQA has a deep authenticity to it. Because this organisation creates the best work of its kind in the world time and time again. If great work matters to you, if you want to contribute great work for great brands, then you might as well work at AKQA."

In conversation with Roger Philby

Roger, Chemistry is famous for its culture. Tell me, is this culture an asset, is it adding to your business value, or is it a driver of profit, or neither?

"Oh, it's an asset, it allows the business to grow without my presence. It's also a P&L contributor because it's our number one differentiator against our competition. What our clients tell us all the time is 'Your IP is probably really cool but the difference is (1) your intent, which is cultural, and (2) your people are incredible. They're amazing. What they do, when they do it, is amazing.'

"That's culture. It's an asset because it allows the company to scale beyond me; it's an asset because if we ever opened another office it will allow that office to be as amazing as this office, that's an asset. It's P&L because it has definitely won us revenue and it drives retention. In all our years we have only lost one client and that was because we misjudged our capacity and screwed up. Once. That is the only client who is not trading with us or has not traded with us since. Our client sustainability is incredible and we are carrying out live projects with 18 of the FTSE 100.

"And so, yes, culture is a huge asset!"

Would you say you actively invest in your culture?

"Absolutely. We call it the energy budget. So, we have a line in the P&L which is energy, which is culture. That number for this year is £48,000, spent just on sustaining the culture of the business. That doesn't include development and training."

Who's responsible for culture?

"Ultimately, every employee is responsible for the culture. The lady who is in charge of making sure that this happens and it's sustained is our Head of Amazing, Lorraine."

And she has Head of Amazing written on her business card?

"Yes. It's her job title."

You mentioned intent as one of the key reasons customers choose you and stay with you. To me that is your big and sustaining why. What is that for Chemistry?

"Our intent is to 'create opportunities for everyone to be brilliant at work.' As you walk in our office it says 'prepare to be brilliant' and then across the office wall at the ceiling height it has 'creating opportunities for everyone to be brilliant at work,' that's our cultural intent. It's why people work here and not anywhere else. What our competitors do is to sell psychometric tests. But we're a *why* company; we create opportunities for everyone to be brilliant at work.

"We do not believe that businesses are run optimally today. They are not run the right way. They are run for the P&L and not for the employees. And we believe that employees are the root of all value. They're the root of all our IP, they're the root of your entire decision making, and they're the root of everything. And if I'm going to go to the market place and say that and sit in front of the CEO and say 'I think it's disgraceful that you spend less than 10%

of your time working on your people and your culture' then I have to spend more time thinking and talking about our people than any other organisation I've been in. That's why we spent that £48,000 on energy. By the way, we've already said the budget for energy has to go up next year."

And what do you spend it on?

"We spend it on a nutritionist. We spend it on feeding everyone. We spend it on thoughtfulness sessions. We spend it on skiing trips every year. We spend it on playtime Friday which is when we get together once a month and play rounders in the park and just hang out. We spend it on the things that keep people going when everything's really quite hard.

"We spend the energy budget on cohesive energy. From eight thirty in the morning to twelve on a Monday is development time. Every employee in the company, including myself, for those three and a half hours, have to be developing themselves. We call it Opportunity To Be Brilliant (OTBB)."

What's the context for all that? What one word defines that activity?

"Informed. Curious. My view is that in order for our people to be brilliant and amazing with their customers they have to be brilliant and amazing in themselves. My opinion is that in order for us to solve our customers' problems we have to have an opinion. My view is you get your opinion from gathering information and working on yourself.

"So my view is that when I send Amy, who's 25-years-old, into a corporate organisation on her day rate she's got to be absolutely amazing. In order for Amy to be able to do that she has to have an opinion, she has to be informed. She has to be articulate, she has to have impact. But more than that she has to have confidence in herself. And OTBB is just about creating the most amazing people that can go out there and do whatever they like."

It's simultaneously stretching them and creating a sense of mastery in the Dan Pink sense of the word? Self-satisfaction and personal development, from which comes confidence.

"Yeah, absolutely."

Tell me about Head of Amazing, what she does.

"So Lorraine's very well paid and her sole job is to ensure that every one of our employees believes they can do their best work here, that they are amazing and they're the best they can be. I view every employee as a volunteer – I'm lucky to have them here. So Lorraine runs the OTBB sessions, she works with our Marketing Goddess to submit awards (we won the Business Enabler of the Year in 2012 and we were in Istanbul last week where we were voted best employer in the UK by the European Business Awards panel which put us in the top ten in Europe – that's a pretty stellar thing for a company of 28 people in Binfield), she runs our employment satisfaction work to find out how people are feeling.

"So, for example, when we realised we were all a bit knackered, she thought 'What can we do about that? A nutritionist.' And bringing in that nutritionist is in the top five things we've done that have fundamentally changed the performance of this business. She's responsible for, two years later, our people and their families still making the same choices around food and they feel great.

"She's also responsible for our Recognition Cards. Our values of Passion, Bravery and Humanity are sustained in this business through the use of Recognition Cards. They manifest themselves in social media so if I open up the chatter stream for today you'll see people getting recognised all the time by colleagues for the great stuff they're doing. Either they've been passionate, brave or human.

"And then Lorraine curates all of that into a presentation so that every Monday we have something called the Magic Meeting at which we spend 45 minutes celebrating the previous week. It's a celebration of where the revenue in the pipeline is, it's a celebration of what we've done in marketing and it's also a celebration of all the recognition cards that were given out the previous week."

So Head of Amazing is responsible for Culture?

"Yes. But having said that, everyone is responsible for culture; as the custodian of the intent I set the tone and my leadership team, through their behaviour, is responsible for sustaining it. You know, it's the north star of the compass.

"I've always said I love Apple as an organisation. Sure, I like some of the products but the reason I love Apple is because whenever you ask them why they did something, they go 'Because it was the best product.'

"Tim Cook [Apple CEO] was interviewed and someone said 'Samsung are beating your arse' and, you know, he just smiled and said 'At what?' And they went 'Well, they're selling more phones than you.' And he responded 'Did I ever say I wanted to sell more phones than Samsung? What have I always said? I want to build a great product and 600m people have bought an iOS product to date so I think we're doing OK.' And I just love this kind of north star thing, build great products don't get distracted by all the other shit, just build great products."

Source leads to outcome: income follows asset?

"Yes. And, the guy was going 'Why don't you build a bigger one, a fatter one?' and Tim goes 'Because it's not great. We've looked at building a bigger phone, and we've built one, and we looked at it and it ain't great so we won't do it. I could fit all our products on this one desk but they're great. Samsung would need to fill a room and how many of those products are great?'

"And I think that's true at Chemistry. We have a cultural intent. For some people that won't be right but for the right people it absolutely is the right place."

And what do you do around here, Roger?

"My job is the custodian of the intent. And I thought lead."

Do you think customers have to deserve to work with you?

"No! So that's not true, it's not an arrogance thing. It's a desire to achieve the outcome for the customer. What we don't want to do is fail. There are customers where we've just gone 'Look, it's not going to work because what you want is to spend £150,000 to tick a box and, whilst we'd love your money, what we care about is the ultimate outcome for you and we don't believe it's going to work.'

"We walked away from a piece of work with a large global company last week because the way they wanted to work was completely inappropriate. They were going to make decisions on human beings with data that we knew you couldn't make those decisions with. So we explained we were refusing to deliver this service for this outcome. It would have been like Apple producing a plastic phone because someone said 'It's not really important that it's great I just want to sell a bunch of cheap phones.'

"What's really interesting about that is that I wasn't the decision maker. The decision maker was one of our consultants who said 'This is what I'm going to do, Roger, I need to tell you because I think we might lose £243,000 worth of revenue.' He was just informing me what they were doing. He just said, this is what I intend to do."

Your culture creates excellence, confidence; and the outcome of that is that people make brave decisions?

"Yes."

Based on an intention and a source rather than an outcome?

"Yes."

And then inform you that you're going to lose quarter of a million quid because it's the right thing to do.

"Yep."

They don't ask your permission that it's right?

"No."

This culture is a magnet which draws customers or at least discriminates customers, and draws talent presumably, do people ring up and go "I'd like to work for you?"

"Yes. So, our two lead consultants are both from a top FTSE, and they both rang up and said we've heard about you, we'd like to work for you. We get more exceptional people wanting to work here than we could possibly hire."

Do you pay more or less than market rate? Does it matter?

"I see salary as a 'base element' on Maslow's hierarchy of needs. We always pay more than they were on before but the way we do pay is by asking what they need. In order for me to have your mind 100% here I need you to hit self-actualisation more often than not. In order to do that I need to remove any concern you may have in your life about money, so the way we pay people is whatever it takes for them not to think about it.

"And when you have the next thing in your life you need to do, you come to us and you discuss it and we remove the need to think about it from a burden perspective. So, for example, a young member of the team needed £800 for a car deposit. So we paid the £800. I look at it and go £800 to us is nothing, it's a drop in the ocean, to her at that time it was huge. So my view on pay and salary is about people being free from the thought of it.

"Now, what I would say is that there's a balance here. There's a reason for our culture. When new people start I do this session, which I call 'The Shit No One Tells You.' So I say, look, we have a nutritionist, we have an amazing culture, we have an amazing intent, you want to work here because of it. We have a Head of Amazing. We go skiing. We take you on trips abroad, we have play time Friday. We do all of this really cool stuff. However, by 7.30am this office is buzzing. I can log in at any time of night and I will see my colleagues working, quite literally any time, and if you ever don't pick up your phone, even on a Sunday afternoon and it's your client or your colleague, we will fire you. That's what our culture means.

"I remember once Alan, our accountant, came and sat in the office for a day and I wasn't here, and he rang me at seven o'clock thinking he was doing me a favour saying, 'Roger, we really need to talk. I don't think your guys are working.' I was really entertained by this so I was like 'Right Alan, tell me about your insight into my culture and the working standards of my business.'

"He said, 'I was in there all day today and all they did was talk.'

"'That's really interesting, Alan, what do you mean?'

"'Some of the time they were pratting about, off in little groups, laughing and joking. I don't know when they get any work done.'

"And I said 'Alan, are you online? How many of your employees are online?'

"He said, 'Well, they've all gone home.' I said, 'Right, do you know how many of mine are online?' I pulled up Google and I could see six of them right at that moment. That'll be nine by nine-ten o'clock, it's probably because they're having dinner and stuff.

"I said, 'What time's your office open, Alan?'

"'Oh, nine, nine thirty.'

"I said, 'Right, mine's open by seven thirty. The truth is Alan, my people don't stop working, they don't see – and this is the big difference Alan – they don't see a difference between what they do in their social life and what they're doing at work. They don't care, it's interchangeable. And the great thing about that, Alan, is when they come into my work they bring all of themselves, not the bit they bring from nine 'til five. They bring the whole lot and do you know what, as a leader that can be quite frustrating sometimes because they want to talk about some shit I don't want them to talk about because I want them to talk about work, right? But you either trust in the system and the culture or you don't. So whilst I thank you for your feedback I am going to disregard it.'

"And my point to him was I get 24 hours of everything of them and the eight hours when they're productive might not be the eight hours I can see but I trust that I get whatever the hours they need to get the job done."

Is he still your accountant?

"No."

In conversation with Frank Bastow

Frank, you run a building firm. This is not perhaps an industry known for its culture. Is culture important to you?

"Oh, most definitely."

Why?

"It makes the energy great and you can overcome lots of obstacles. Instead of people going 'That's going to destroy us,' or whatever, everybody's got a positive attitude and they all work together to overcome it. And it's taken us through this bad time, you know? You should come to our pizza nights! Once a month we have pizza nights. We do a little coaching and then we'll get beer and pizzas in and we're talking, drinking, laughing and the whole firm's in the thing. We have our family picnic days, too, stuff like that. I love it."

Do you invest in this culture?

"For sure."

What kind of investment?

"We like getting awards. That's a context for everything – if we've done something brilliantly, we end up getting awards. We won a Considerate Constructors Award (and remember the firms we are competing against are multi-million pound businesses). Out of 6500 jobs in the whole country, we were in the top five. We do stuff like planting trees in local schools, putting suntan cream on the top roof for the scaffolders or the roofers to use so they don't get burnt... Helping, you know? Just making London a more beautiful place and getting people involved. Love all that stuff."

And has the culture changed over the years? Are you conscious of having to manage the process of change?

"It's tougher to run culture when it's a hard economy. We love spending money on doing fun stuff. We've worked out ways of doing that on a lot less money. You don't have to fly everyone out to Florence or Las Vegas to have a good time (like we have in the past). We can bring our own food, go over to Richmond Park and knock up a barbecue ourselves and have a laugh. Even when the gazebo blows away in a force 9 gale! Nurturing a great culture doesn't need to be expensive."

You mention making London beautiful. Is that the intent of the firm?

"'Making London beautiful' is our positioning. What we say publicly. Our intent is to nurture everybody... and that knocked a lot of people when we drove that through!"

For a building company, I bet.

"To nurture, yeah. We had a problem explaining it to some of our clients, too. But, there are individual surveyors who appreciate and understand 'to nurture', and they also understand our values of brave, harmonious and true. Harmonious doesn't mean that we all go around like priests. Harmonious can even mean that we're all arguing – but we do it together, in harmony. We are in tune with each other. On the same page."

This means you've defined those values?

"Yes."

What does brave mean?

"Brave means letting other people be brave in the organisation. For example, the quieter ones, the more reserved ones – if they've got something to contribute (and they have some great ideas), they can't get the ideas out if you keep on shouting above them. You have to make them brave, to come out and you have to encourage them. We've taken out all the blockages in our organisation. So if somebody is a labourer in our business and they want to be the managing director, they have the path and the ability to do it. Nobody will stop them from going that way.

"And as long as you're making London beautiful, we say you have the right to go off, even if it's not commercial, and do something that makes London beautiful. When we had the riots, our site agents just wanted to go up to Clapham with the brushes and start cleaning the streets, it was just a natural thing to do – it doesn't matter about the time or cost."

It sounds like you give complete responsibility within a context. How have you achieved that?

"We have a broad employment contract so it's not specific tasks, it's all very contextual. And it stands out like a sore thumb if people aren't going the extra mile or they're not being creative. Everybody else notices, and they'll go and discuss with the person – 'Why aren't you doing this?' It's not because they think that they're lazy or whatever, it's because they don't understand why the person's not enjoying their job as much as they are. You should be proud. You should feel proud of what you're doing.

"And it means I don't have to run the show anymore. They do. And that makes it a far more valuable business. And it allows me to go and build even more value elsewhere. In a family building business like mine, you'd normally work out how much your business is worth based on 90% of what your sales are if you're not in the business any more. In the old days, I WAS the business. If I wasn't in the business it'd be worth nothing at that time. But do you know what happened to me the other day? To show you how much this focus on asset has changed everything. I was walking to Cundy Street, SW1, right? Million and a half pound job, and there's a surveyor there I've never met before. I realised as I was walking up, 'Do you know what? I'm irrelevant here.' And it made me feel proud.

"My Dad, if he felt he was irrelevant, he would have been terrified, he believed that he had to be better than everybody else in the firm. That was a really expensive lie that he lived. Now, the firm runs by itself. I'm so confident, right, 'cos I have left the business alone for a year. I left them to do their own thing and I believed that if I left it a year not only would it still be around, it would be a stronger business. And I was absolutely right!"

In conversation with Russell Stinson

Russell, your business is in providing essential services to the five-star hospitality industry in London. This is a world of fierce price competition, minimum wages and high staff turnover. What place has culture in your business?

"I think from day one we'd taken a look at what we'd done previously and where we really felt the opportunity was to get things right. We wanted to build a great company but we understood that we could only do it if we had the right mixture of looking after people and of giving opportunity to people to help us deliver a great service to the client. And, for me, too many people – too many companies – were missing out the opportunity to develop their staff and give opportunity to their staff, coach and develop their staff, because it's an industry of low wages and one of the things that staff massively appreciate is coaching, training, and giving opportunity to them to progress their careers.

"It's that internal development that's allowed us to bring people from the first day they moved into the company to supervisors to operations managers to trainers to kind of coaches within the bigger sites. And all of that has allowed us to provide a better service and our clients think we've got the best staff."

"But it's not happened by accident because they're taken from the same pool of people as all the competition. Within their communities we are seen as a good company to go and work for, and if you take a look at our front office we don't advertise but we've got between ten and thirty people coming in to register on a daily basis. That's created a company now with 1300 staff. Essentially if we needed a hundred staff tomorrow we'd just need to talk to our current staff and we will have them to start training tomorrow. One of the biggest secrets has been looking after our staff as best we can, we can't obviously pay people £20 an hour but it's getting the basics right of developing them that counts far more."

Opportunity for what Dan Pink calls mastery?

"Sure. Three of our operations managers started off in our business as either kitchen porters or night cleaners. Looking after our people – respecting them – is the secret of our scale. We've doubled every year in size since we started. These are significant jumps but that growth has always been through developing people. Without getting the culture and the people side of it right we would never have been able to sustain that level of growth."

So culture here is driving recruitment, driving retention of quality staff. But is it also driving acquisition and retention of clients?

"Without a doubt. I think I mentioned earlier the incestuous nature of hospitality; head chefs, executive chefs, food and beverage directors, they all know each other, they all grew up within the industry. They tend to know and use the best people based on reputation, based on relationship. We work very hard on that. There's a big relationship aspect of it but for me it's all built on a foundation of providing a great service. Without that a relationship will not go anywhere."

Chapter 5.
The Nelson Touch?

"I rely far more on gut instinct than researching huge amounts of statistics."

Sir Richard Branson

"Leadership is simply about getting people to do something they wouldn't normally feel able to do."

Commodore Jerry Kyd RN

CLEARLY CULTURE IS BASED ON GREAT LEADERSHIP, BUT leadership itself is one of those abstract concepts that is endlessly debated and keeps business writers and publishers lucratively busy.

Yet for the CEO of an entrepreneurial business I think leadership is actually pretty simple (although not easy).

To begin with, leadership can be defined in three phases, which I'll go on to look at in turn below:

1. Set the context

2. Manage the energy

3. Coach don't play

Seeing the wood for the trees

There's a modern urban legend I rather enjoy that is said to be the transcript of a radio conversation between two vessels:

> Would the vessel 24 miles north-east of Danger Point steer 20°
> to starboard to avoid a collision. Over.

Vessel hailing us, I suggest you steer 20° to starboard to avoid a collision. Over.

Sir, this is most urgent, you must immediately steer 20° to starboard to avoid an imminent collision. Over.

This is the USS Enterprise, *the most powerful surface vessel on the face of the earth and, I believe, I can require you to steer 20° to starboard.*

Sir, this is a lighthouse. It's your decision.

For all sorts of reasons this exchange never, of course, happened. It is, however, a great example of context.

View from the helicopter

As a leader, setting the context for your organisation is one of your most vital functions. The right context enables you to set the strategic direction and allow your team to deliver operationally – whilst your time and energy is freed up to pursue growth and scale. It allows you to take a broader, helicopter view which should allow you to spot threats and opportunities that will be hidden if you stay in the content with your team. As Ajaz Ahmed says:

> "As a leader, you have to make sure that the right ideas win, not the politics or the hierarchy."

Getting clarity on your *context* will also give you the basis for making swift and efficient decisions. You must be decisive even if you are uncertain. Sometimes you will be wrong, but as John F. Kennedy shrewdly observed:

> "There are risks and costs to a program of action. But they are far less than the long-range risks and costs of comfortable inaction."

It can be tough to make decisions as the leader, particularly in a private business when you have to make choices with little information.

Then you must have confidence in your convictions. Trust your instincts – they will often be right. As Ajaz Ahmed and Stefan Olander comment in *Velocity*, "have the balls to make the calls." It is absolutely right to take soundings and manage collaboratively but ultimately it's down to you if a decision has to be made. To quote Ajaz and Stefan again, "no good joke survives a committee of six."

Steve Jobs once said about running Apple, "never let the noise of other people's opinions drown out your own inner voice." Commodore Jerry Kyd RN, who I interview at length in this chapter, concurs, saying of his experience as Captain of HMS *Ark Royal* and HMS *Illustrious*:

> "I learnt that when emergencies did happen, and they did, actually your intuition is pretty good. If you run with your instincts, nine times out of ten your instinct is right. Particularly if you've been in that business for a while, the first thought that comes into your head tends to be the right one. Before you discard your first intuitive thought be very careful because normally it's the right one."

It's interesting that in this quote Jerry Kyd uses the phrase "particularly if you've been in that business for a while." In other words your experience allows you to set the right context.

Acting on instinct will not mean you are alone. In a PRWeek/Burson-Marsteller survey of CEOs, 62% rated *gut feel* as being highly influential in their business decisions. In my experience this *gut feel* is particularly prevalent in owner-managers and entrepreneurs.

The corollary of this is that if your view of your business is not sufficiently contextual then you can easily get stuck in your own content and your own beliefs. You will find effective decision-making hard. Your organisation won't innovate and may not grow. Certainly when things change you will be caught out (see Chapter 7).

If you allow your belief that you are in the most powerful surface vessel on the face of the globe to set the context for your decisions then you will refuse to accept another reality. Until that reality is a lighthouse at which point you look a bit of a prat. Context allows for flexibility. But is has to be the right context.

Longing for the endless immensity of the sea

I have already introduced setting the context at a high level – setting the *why* as a clear intent and inspiring your people with your dream. I quoted Reed Hastings of Netflix in the previous chapter. Hastings has built a great culture and leads a highly successful, innovative and high-value business based on an understanding of how to lead creative and innovative people to allow them to perform at their optimum. "The best leaders," he says, "figure out how to get great outcomes by setting the appropriate context, rather than by trying to control their people."

If you set the appropriate context and give talented people the autonomy to act within it you will be amazed at the results. Once again, this presupposes your people are sufficiently talented, but we'll come to that later.

Ajaz Ahmed is clear on this:

"Find and attract people that share the same values, and give them the freedom to unleash their imagination and do the best work of their lives. If you hire good people, you have to let them make decisions. We have zero committees at AKQA and an entrepreneurial environment which means decision-making is as autonomous as it can be. Hire good people who share your values, provide clarity in what needs to be done, trust them and give them independence to do their jobs."

Antoine de Saint-Exupéry – the French poet and author – framed this concept rather lyrically when he said:

"If you want to build a ship, don't drum up people to collect wood and don't assign them tasks and work, but rather teach them to long for the endless immensity of the sea."

Put more prosaically, as a leader your task is to set *the context* and not manage the *content*.

As an example of how this works, when Reed Hastings is asked about the vacation policy at Netflix (and remember this is a large and complex multinational organisation) he says, "there is no vacation policy or tracking. There is also no clothing policy at Netflix, but no one comes to work naked."

Context comes in layers. It is obviously about setting the big picture; the dream. It is equally about setting the key strategic direction and framework for this and the next stage of the business. It is about setting the framework for decisions in the long and short term. And communicating that clearly to your team.

I learnt a great tip from Kevin Roberts, the CEO of Saatchi & Saatchi. Kevin's approach is to rigorously set ten key priorities – and only ten – that you will actually deliver in the next 100 days and talk about those to your team. This concept of *10 things in 100 days* is easy to communicate and easier to deliver, it also tends to force you to stay in context and not content. I have used that to run my businesses, report to my board and communicate with our team ever since.

Forgetting Sheila's daughter's wedding

So what of the second key aspect of business leadership, *managing the energy*? This should be the constant task of the leader in any organisation.

I recently met Bryan Raven who runs a fast-growing lighting specialist called White Light. Bryan told me he writes a short email as a kind of blog to all his staff every day. It is the first thing he does in the morning. Every day without fail. This is Bryan's approach to managing energy.

As the leader of the business this role never ends. It requires your constant attention. This is not an easy thing to do. Of course, you are allowed a day off. But you are not allowed an off day.

We're all familiar with seeing sports or performance stars who sweep past fans waiting patiently for an autograph. Perhaps they are having a bad day but we imagine we would never behave like that if we were lucky enough to be in their position. However, most of us behave like that only too often. We're stressed, late or distracted, and sweep through the office in our own world. We ignore staff, forget it was Sheila's daughter's wedding last week, etc. This is a failure to manage the energy of our team.

Uncomfortable though it may be for us as entrepreneurs, our team expects us to inspire them. To allow them to always be their BEST requires you to manage their energy – and not the other way round.

On the touchline

Last of the three elements of leadership, what of *coach don't play*? That simply means you acknowledge that you are not on the field anymore. You have created a culture of real autonomy in your people which allows you to support and develop their mastery.

Best of all, this starts to create a business independent of you, a business with saleable value, and it frees up your time to focus your energy and talents on making your business assets a reality.

I mentioned in the previous chapter that leadership was the key ingredient in getting my climbing companions and me up Aconcagua. This was, after all, not a military operation, so our leader could not command and compel. Rather like the CEO, his role was to inspire, instil confidence and create in us the belief that we could, as a team, achieve the goal.

Reflecting afterwards on the attributes this man showed, I recognised his skills in setting a clear context, not just for the whole expedition but for that day or that stage. He was also adept at managing our energy. It felt that he knew us as individuals and adapted his style to how we felt and what we needed day by day and hour by hour. Most fundamentally, he created a sense of empowering belief that the goal could be achieved.

I recall reading comments from a member of Shackleton's expedition that, even as the Endurance sank beneath the ice leaving them marooned on pack ice thousands of miles from home and with little rational hope of survival, the leadership qualities of "the Boss" were such that they never once doubted that they would get home alive. That is leadership. That is the art of inspiring others to be more than they believe they can be.

The Alchemist's view

In conversation with Frank Bastow

Frank, how would you describe your leadership style and what you've learnt over the years?

"The biggest thing I've learned is to get a context and to drive it through your organisation. If you can agree on the context it's easier to drive through with less push back. If you've got focused and simple visions in a context, everybody understands what they have to do. They understand that they're building a house not just building its walls or putting windows in – they can see the whole picture.

"So I guess my leadership style is empowering, building the confidence of others. Uncovering and polishing the diamonds hidden away inside them. I do it and then they do it. And that gives me freedom. The freedom to get on with other stuff. To build value."

In conversation with Rupert Lee-Browne

Rupert, tell me about leadership at Caxton.

"This is where the journey's interesting because the original management style that I adopted was not exactly pleasant. The management techniques that I learnt in the late eighties in a very tough buying environment were not ideal. I suppose, like a number of entrepreneurs, my management style has not been great but what I did recognise is that in order for us to grow significantly my style needed to change."

When did you realise that?

"Five to six years ago. And that's why I employed Jane Emma as Director of People because I knew that we needed better management skills in the business. It was the realisation that we'd had five years of a revolving door of good people. I wanted to stem the flow of good people out the door which was politely pointed out to me as being my fault. Fine. So let's change that. Let's make sure we have the right people coming into the business, that they are expertly managed and motivated to stay and do an amazing job. This is about managing people properly and that included teaching me and all the leaders in the business how to manage people properly. It took me a long time to understand it but it's all about the people."

In conversation with Commodore Jerry Kyd RN

As a contrast to the usual interviews with well-known business leaders, I thought I would share a conversation I had with Commodore Jerry Kyd RN to put a quite different perspective on organisational leadership. Look out for references to setting the context, managing the energy and coaching rather than playing.

Jerry, I would be really interested to get your perspective on leadership and how your experience of leading in a military environment might lend useful insight to those leading in commercial organisations. Before we get into that can you tell me a bit about your career to date?

"Well, I joined the Royal Navy as a Warfare Officer in 1985 and I spent most of my early career as a junior officer at sea learning my trade in various ships, including carriers, frigates and destroyers in home waters and around the world. In my late twenties, I specialised as a Navigation Officer and a Gunnery Officer with increasing levels of responsibility for the ships' fighting and sea going capability. A key capability, of course, is the crew, and from your very first appointment as a very junior officer you are charged with the welfare and training of people. Very rapidly, you learn that leadership and management is an art rather than a science!

"After various appointments as a sea going officer, I was promoted to the rank of Commander RN in 2004 at the age of 35 and blessed with my own frigate command, HMS *Monmouth*. A huge responsibility and a huge privilege. For a Naval officer, ship command is the highlight of their career. A half billion pound asset, several hundred crew under your command focuses the mind! But it is your ship, you are the Captain, the responsibility is entirely yours and this brings pleasure and pain, not least worry and stress at times.

"Being at the top is often a lonely place to be. After my frigate command time I spent a number of years in the Ministry of Defence including serving as a personal Staff Officer to the Chief of Defence Staff, the professional head of the UK Armed Forces and the primary military advisor to the Prime Minister. This was an exquisitely fascinating time, seeing the strategic leadership level across government and the fascinating parallels with tactical leadership on the shop floor.

"From there I was promoted to Captain RN and assumed command of the strike aircraft carrier HMS *Ark Royal* in 2010, before moving to another carrier, HMS *Illustrious*, operating in the amphibious assault role with embarked Royal Marines. In 2012, I took up my present appointment as the Captain of the Britannia Royal Naval College, training 450 young naval officers every year from 27 different countries.

"It is hugely invigorating and inspiring to see how motivated and able the young generation are. The average age is 22 and they are very well educated, inquiring and motivated. To see them blossom, particularly in beginning the long process to hone and develop their potential to lead and manage others through BRNC's Royal Naval Leadership Academy. The key is to identify potential and then develop it in a style that suits your organisation, its ethos and its outputs.

"So my career's been varied and I've been really privileged to have held many command positions over the last 30 years, leading and managing large, complex teams in challenging situations. It is very true that you never stop learning! Of course, personal development is driven by experiences, particularly learning from the inevitable mistakes as well as when things go well. In the Navy, career progression is tied to increasingly challenging leadership complexity as you go up the ranks but the continuity of the Naval career system prepares you extremely well, not least in inculcating the right values and ethos that ultimately drives a large organisation."

Tell me more about leadership. Am I right in thinking that, contextually, leadership in a military sense has many parallels with leadership in civilian life? That being responsible for a body of men and women in an aircraft carrier has similarities with being in charge of a business?

"Before I try and offer an answer to that specific question, be wary of anyone telling you that they're an expert leader. In my opinion, such people are extremely rare. There are plenty of expert leadership theorists, academics, authors and commentators who add much value to the subject but we can only draw credible conclusions and develop leadership skills properly from real experiences in the real world with real people. And here is the central point common to all leaders: it is the aim of leadership, whether you are dealing with people in a business or indeed in an aircraft carrier, to motivate and direct people – to get things done. For the Navy, and I daresay for any civilian firm, getting things done is aimed squarely at two outcomes: winning and serving the aims of the organisation.

"All leaders should ask themselves when presented with tough decisions: what is the best thing to do in the interests of the company? This question will invariably lead you to making the right decision and issuing the right direction and guidance. That is common to both military and business leaders. Success may not be guaranteed from good leadership, but it stacks the odds very heavily in your favour. A well-lead, cohesive, motivated team is much stronger than the sum of its parts. Root out non-team playing attitudes and behaviours swiftly; a bad apple can ruin the best barrel quickly, particularly in high-energy or quick-moving organisations or when the pressure is on.

"Good leadership is critical for driving activity and success but we must be careful here who we see as leaders. In the Navy we inculcate a sense of responsibility for the organisation from the bottom up. We actively promote the view that anyone, whatever level, can exercise some leadership, particularly at the tactical, day-to-day level. In this sense, leadership is the obligation of the many not the prerogative of the few. For example, if the youngest sailor on board finds a fire in a compartment or an injured crewman I expect them to take charge of the situation and do what is right without waiting for orders.

"Empowerment and delegation should be instinctive in any vibrant, agile organisation and breeds well-being and confidence in the work force. People who feel they can make a difference and are trusted and valued by their managers will always go the extra mile for you. The trouble is there is a great temptation by leaders to keep control because they want to control outcomes. But this is a false economy in the long run because you will de-motivate and reduce moral; empower and delegate within the bounds of common sense against clear aims and let them get on with it. The results can be startling. In the military we call this Mission Command."

Most people would assume that the difference between leadership in the military and leadership in civilian life is that you can compel people to obey.

"Well, in the military we have to obey orders – basic discipline is essential for fighting efficiency and this is legally bound under the Naval Discipline Act. But real-life leadership in the 21st century Navy is much more sophisticated than simply issuing orders. We can perhaps define effective leadership at its most basic as the ability to get others to willingly do things that they normally would really rather *not* do. To do so well demands a suite of personal qualities, characteristics and ingredients that are far more complex than just barking orders.

"The British military is a volunteer force of very capable, hard-working people who need to be actively managed in a team environment that sets the right behaviours in individuals that compels them to give their best in order to serve the interests of the organisation or task at hand. This is as true in the civilian sphere as it is in a warship. My only caveat is where heroic or inspirational leadership is required in the extreme situation of imminent danger in war or crisis where quick, sharp and clear orders are essential. However, across all these scenarios, the essential ingredients of credibility, emotional intelligence, confidence, ability to communicate, effective intelligence and niche professional knowledge are common attributes in an effective leader.

"You have to learn to trust yourself and your experience. I have already said that leadership, as a Captain of a ship, as an MD or CEO, can be a very lonely spot, particularly when things are not going well. You have to have the resilience and strength to drive on even when others below are flagging. It is human nature in tough times to look at the leader for direction and answers to woes. There is nothing easier than leading and motivating others when the going is easy, profits are rolling in and the share price is sky-bound. But you earn your pay when things go wrong; then it is your backbone, personality, drive, energy, moral courage and decision-making abilities that will decide success or failure. Trust your instincts too – they are normally right! This is all common to civilian or military environments.

"That said, I think that the military is probably unique in that we more often have situations that demand leadership in acute situations: a missile is inbound, a serious fire, an aircraft crash and so on. These extreme situations demand a *directive and subjective* leadership style: 'You, Bloggs, do this now!' Military people obey immediately, not just from a raw discipline reason but because they already know, trust and respect you as a leader. You must know your people, and they must know you too. Acute situations call for the leader to stand up to the plate and take charge. To demur is an abrogation of your responsibilities as a leader. Again, tough choices mean tough decisions."

What happens the rest of the time?

"For the vast majority of the time we all use a *consultative and objective* leadership style, where you involve and seek the team's expertise, advice and input to achieve targets. You are looking for the team to be part of the solution, to help you decide on the best course of action. They may proffer the crucial fact or issue that you have missed and which may fundamentally influence your final decision, orders and direction. Staff love it because they feel valued and needed. But leadership is not a democracy! At the end of the day you must take responsibility for the decisions and the outcomes of those decisions, so don't be bullied!

"In all of this human dynamic, any successful and effective leader, whether in business or in the military, has to have well-developed emotional intelligence. We are playing a complex people game here, sometimes for high odds and significant risk and it is people who will be the solution. The ability to gauge the situation and gauge the immediate team you're working with is critical. A well-tuned emotional understanding of what makes people tick and their concerns is hugely important. A leader must be a real person who sees individuals in a team and not just the holistic whole. Of course, this comes easier, normally, as you get older and more experienced, but coaching and mentoring young leaders in understanding emotional issues is vital."

In all of those situations you have individuals in immediate danger. What is it that inspires or motivates those people to put themselves in danger?

"Well, I think that's a good question because everyone has different motivations and values. Many people will say that in the military it is simply about following orders. But that is only part of the answer why a rational human being willingly places himself in acute danger. They must respect the officer, trust their leadership and believe in the aim of the moment for the common good. And here I think is the key to your question; people will do amazing things when they believe in the cause and for the collective benefit of a team they feel part of.

"In the military, we actively build small units of people into bonded teams who are moulded together, navigate adversity together and who collectively believe in their leadership and in what they are doing. Indeed, so strong is this team spirit that men and women in the British Armed Forces willingly lay down their lives for each other and for their cap badge, ship or Regiment. This is about inculcating common aims, ethos and an unselfish environment where reward comes to those who display altruistic tendencies for the good of the organisation. The me culture is damaging, the us culture is what you want."

Ah, so now we have a team with a shared purpose. Clearly direction is important but the reason you put yourself in danger is something to do with the team. With the culture that team has created?

"Culture in any team or organisation is hugely important. Building and nurturing a group of individuals into a team is absolutely vital. As I have said, it is critically important that everyone understand the aims of the organisation. For any organisation, everyone in the team should have clearly set objectives and they should be very clear what moral, ethical and behavioural values the company expects. They should morph to the company for the common good, not the other way around.

"Now, of course, I am not saying that individuality is not important, of course it is. But in the same way a rowing eight is made up of individuals, they must all pull on the oars at the same time. Play to people's strengths but make sure they understand the culture of your company. They must all know that no one is more or less important than the person at the top – everyone is key to achieving the aims of the organisation, otherwise they wouldn't be employed! People must know this because it generates corporate pride, identity, team identity and, crucially, a feel-good factor. We call it morale."

So if you're commanding a ship you have to create a sense of group purpose and then you communicate that. What is the purpose of a Royal Navy ship?

"To be ready for operations. It's a flexible, adaptable, sovereign asset that can go and do whatever the government wishes, from maritime security, disaster relief, search and rescue, engaging with countries around the world and supporting British commercial and political interest, and, of course, ultimately war fighting. A Royal Naval ship needs to be ready for all these missions, with the equipment and trained people ready.

"And it's the captain's responsibility to make sure that the ship is ready to turn its hand to whatever's required. A warship is a very expensive and complicated beast, 250 people in a very small metal shell, trained to work and fight together effectively. And again, it comes down to making sure everyone understands fully what his or her role is in making the ship do its job, be operationally capable and meet its objectives."

Which sounds very like a business. What specifically could businesses learn from the military approach to leadership?

"The most important thing in a leader is the necessity to talk to people, about being next to the people you lead, being on the shop floor. I guess that in business it may be harder for leaders to really get to know their people. But whatever the churn or geographic separation, one must have touchstones with the people who ultimately deliver you the results. You must understand what makes people tick in order to lead them effectively. This is easy – go out and talk to them. And it doesn't really matter what about; they will love you for it and your interest in them."

Taking you back to your first command, HMS Monmouth, when you were 35, you said you learnt a lot. What did you learn?

"It taught me the meaning of responsibility and pinnacle leadership – it's yours, no one else's. The results of the ship reflected on me, no one else can be blamed. So I had to think properly about my leadership and how I could play to my strengths and mitigate my weaknesses. Everyone is different and everyone has different leadership styles. It doesn't matter as long as people are motivated to willingly get things done.

"And as the Captain, master and commander, at the top of the tree in a ship, I learnt that I could change people's lives, shape careers, and make things better. Of course, it is very satisfying when things go well but brutal when they don't. With nowhere to hide, you have to live with yourself when your decisions are wrong, as they will inevitably be; everyone is imperfect. You just have to learn and move on and bank the experience."

Presumably running a frigate on operations you are pretty much on your own. There is a theoretical command structure above you but no easy access to advice.

"Modern communications mean that you are never far from your boss but we exercise what in the military we call Mission Command. Mission Command is where the person above you gives the objective that needs to be achieved but leaves you with executive authority to get on and do it with a certain resource and timescale. So I understood the effect that the Admiral wanted me to achieve with my ship and then it was up to me to decide how I was going to achieve it. Equally, I could be saying to a very young 19-year-old Leading Hand, go ashore with a shore party and do something. I gave him mission command with his own responsibilities, with well-defined boundaries. Empower the able and you'll be amazed by what people can achieve."

George Patten used to say "Don't tell people how to do things, tell them what to do and let them surprise you with their results." I've always felt it was even more important to tell them why and let them work out the what and how, which sounds like what you are saying. You're setting the fundamental purpose – the why – but you let them interpret what they're going to do and how they're going to do it.

"Absolutely right. I understood the aims. It was up to me about how I met them. So I might be tasked with interdicting smuggling of drugs or people from Africa to Europe for the slave trade or prostitution rings. But it was up to me to work out a scheme of manoeuvre, a plan, using the assets at my command, helicopters, ships and so forth, to meet the objective set.

"I then delegated bits of the overarching plan to subordinates with clearly articulated objectives and gave them mission command. There is nothing more damaging than trying to micro-manage an operation from miles away. Empowerment and subsequent success, winning if you like, is a very powerful boost for morale and productivity in a team. Everyone wants to do well and be part of a success story. Give them the means and training to do it."

This ability to effectively delegate and not interfere is a skill of leadership?

"Yes, knowing when and to what limit to delegate is crucial. In the Navy, we talk a lot about 'the Nelson Touch' – the ability to sit round a table with your commanders and explain coherently what it is that needs to be achieved and the vision you hold without restricting their operational flexibility to achieve it.

"The genius of the leader is the ability to see a battle-winning plan or strategy and then communicating it so everyone understands the effects you wish to achieve and then empowering people below you to deliver their part of the plan. But you, as the overall leader, must keep a beady eye on progress and step in, but only when required."

As the layman would say, what Nelson is famous for is inspiring people, communicating and then getting out of the way and allowing them to interpret.

"Correct. His famous signal 'no man can do much wrong if he places his ship alongside that of the enemy' is a classic. This is what I want – to smash the enemy. Here is the battle plan, but whatever happens to alter that plan, ultimately I just want you to use your skill and initiative to beat the enemy by bold sailing, fast gun fire and courage."

Allowing them to make command decisions, feeling empowered to make those decisions within a context, within a vision.

"Absolutely. Of course that doesn't mean the leader is then divorced from what happens because he can monitor, he can gauge progress, and he can then set boundaries to the people he's empowered by saying, 'Report to me on a daily or weekly basis. You will be judged against these metrics or against an effect to be achieved.'

"Communication is key. Setting out the company's vision and mission clearly, in a way that is understandable to everyone in plain English is part of this. People need to know how they are contributing to the overarching aims of the organisation, in so doing they are made to feel valued and contributory."

Ok, let me do a quick summary of this. I've heard that leadership is about knowledge of your subject, so you have credibility, and deep knowledge of your people, so you know how to lead them. It's about exercising emotional intelligence and understanding and trusting your intuition. It's about establishing a strong team culture based on shared values and about the 'Nelson Touch', setting a clear purpose or context and powerfully communicating that whilst having the confidence to delegate mission command to allow people to deliver operationally against that context.

"That's a good summation."

I've been listening. In a larger organisation knowing your people as you describe is not always possible. When you were commanding HMS Ark Royal or HMS Illustrious, how many people were on board?

"1200."

And how many people did you know?

"Of course on a very big ship like that, I exercised my day-to-day leadership through my senior leaders on board. On an aircraft carrier, you have a large number of people and so it is impossible to know them all. But I ensured I walked around the ship twice a day and spoke to any junior sailor I passed and it is amazing how quickly what you say reaches every nook of the ship because after a week or two, you have probably spoken to most of the ship's company.

"They often would ask questions that I could put right there and then. It never failed to amaze me how loose tittle-tattle and gossip can be both so inaccurate and damaging and I and my officers could put that right by incessant engagement. But when I was commanding my frigate with 250 people on board, things were much easier. There is no excuse for not knowing this many people well in your organisation. It is useful to get to know the real characters and the people who can get things to work for you; every company has them, they are the makers and shakers. Get them onside early and it will pay dividends. Be straight with them at all times – no bull!"

This suggests that even in a military environment there are lynchpin people? Not necessarily because of their role but because of who they are?

"Correct. Knowing the characters, knowing who can inspire, motivate, who has the equity in the pecking order in the crew, can be most useful. They may not be the people you like the best but when the chips are down, they are the people that will save your bacon.

"There's nothing easier than leading when things are going well and making profits, when you're sailing when the sun's out and it's flat calm water, that's easy. Any fool can do that. It is when something goes wrong very quickly, that's when you need people you can rely on. That's why you need to know who to rely on, who to task, who to promote and who to reward. Of course every organisation is the same – knowing the right people is important."

Tell me more about commanding a huge ship like Ark Royal. *From a leadership perspective what have you learnt?*

"Being the Captain of a frigate or an aircraft carrier is fundamentally the same. You set the pace, the culture, the boundaries and the vision. In many ways the ship is the Captain – if he is slack so will the ship be. Leadership by example should guide one's actions and behaviour.

"Of course the bigger the business the more convoluted it is, not just more complicated. In *Ark Royal* and *Illustrious*, I had a lot of Departments, 1200 people, hundreds of tons of explosives, a large number of aircraft and what is a huge piece of steel to keep safe. In a big organisation, you're much more in the business of setting the culture and overarching direction; you are less in the tactical space. You have more experienced management below you to do the nuts and bolts, so use them, empower them and hold them to account. If you create the right culture, and positively encourage the right behaviours, things will generally be good.

"As the Captain of *Monmouth*, a frigate, I'd been used to knowing everyone intimately but of course in an aircraft carrier you just can't. You can walk round the ship 24 hours a day and still meet new people on week five and, of course, people come and go, like any large organisation. As Captain of a bigger ship, communicating the *main effort* – that is the current priority – to the key managers, the Heads of Departments, was crucial. On a bigger ship you have to adjust to more layers of management and therefore you have to trust more. I said before, once people understand the overriding objective of their ship, what you want to achieve, that must be cascaded down so everyone knows their part to play in serving the aims of the organisation."

Describe communication on a ship of that size then. How do you communicate the main effort?

"In many different ways. *Main efforts* are articulated to focus activity and thinking. This can be for strategic direction, a vision; a medium term, say six monthly directive; or for an acute issue on a particular day.

"Vision and directives are written and then backed up by verbal means, such as my regular Captain's Addresses to the entire ship's company. I tended to write one paragraph for my vision, a one-page document for what I wanted to achieve in the following six months to a year. In all written work, I laid out what I wanted in a way that was pithy and to the point and could be understood by every sailor in plain English. Everyone can write yards of rubbish, the trick is to keep it short and digestible to all.

"On a day-to-day basis, any tactical *main effort* would be generally verbal. For example, if we had a fire onboard the ship's *main effort* would be to contain the incident, tend to the burned and recover the ship, and this would be piped over the ship's tannoy system so that people would know what the priority was. It gives direction for what is at the top of my list.

"Apart from emergencies, every evening the second in command used to make a tannoy call to the whole ship's company that rounded up the day's activities, what had gone right, what had gone wrong and with a bit of humour. It's also important that, had things gone wrong in the day, then we accept that, we learn our lessons and we move on.

"There is nothing worse for a subordinate than not knowing what your boss thinks of you. That is one of the absolute cardinal sins of leadership; lacking the moral courage to give honest feedback. If people are underperforming they must be told clearly where they are failing and regularly as well and how they can improve. There's no point holding out for the annual appraisal because it will come as a shock and it will just demotivate everyone.

"But also, it was really important to say 'this went really well' and giving a lot of praise and feedback. People below you love feedback. People love it when they are recognised. So it doesn't have to be a prize or present or money, it's recognition and that's important. But you can't do the whole thing yourself. You must empower your management. If you continually go direct to the shop floor to provide direct feedback that can undermine your management team so you've got to be very careful. There's a balancing act, as always. This is why a leader has to be emotionally intelligent. He has to observe; it's not just what you're looking at, it's what you see that's most important."

May I ask you about the period when Ark Royal *was taken out of service? Most people will recall* Ark Royal *being decommissioned and that was under your command. That must have been a moment of crisis.*

"It was a very difficult moment. I'd served on the ship for three tours so she's very close to my heart. So literally when you are told your ship is being scrapped and your company are going to be disbanded within weeks it's extraordinarily difficult, very emotional. My word, does it put you on the spot as a leader, because suddenly you have to balance looking after and managing the crew, whilst managing the issue against the bigger picture. In this case, the government had made decisions based on a Defence Review that involved a number of very difficult decisions.

"The ship's company had worked for years to keep the ship at peak operational capability – they were proud. They were extremely angry at seeing the ship taken out of service. I had to manage this charged atmosphere, empathise but also ensure we remained dignified and professional in those last weeks. In unforeseen circumstances, particularly where people's livelihoods are affected, you have to force yourself to be as circumspect and balanced as possible. You must show leadership in loyalty to the powers that have made the decision, whatever your own personal views, whilst showing respect for the concerns and emotions of your people. It is tough!

"It is at these sorts of times that you are glad you know and understand your people and that hopefully your rapport with them, mutual respect and credibility will see you through. But always be honest with them – there is nothing worse for a leader's stock than false platitudes and half-truths. Have the moral courage to say it as it is, however difficult. Otherwise, they will just believe the front pages of *The Sun* over you."

And 48 hours later, you then became public spokesman for the decision. Interviewed by global media.

"Correct. Then you have to understand what's in the best interest of the Royal Navy. To stand in front of the camera in that situation and criticise the decision of my Admiral would have been absolutely wrong. The Navy goes on. Every company and every business makes decisions that people on the shop floor don't like, often because they don't have the full context of why a decision has been made, but it has to happen.

"That's what leadership is all about, getting people to do things they would not normally want to do. I didn't want to tell my ship's company that my ship was being scrapped but I could see the bigger picture... Very, very difficult. Probably my greatest leadership challenge in my career. There you go. Time heals."

Chapter 6.
No-one Dies of a Frickin' Heart Attack on My Set

"Your best people are very much the ones who just get it, feel it, know what you stand for and personify what it's all about."

Keith Abel

"My job is to champion those values and ensure that we create a culture of excellence where mediocrity is not tolerated and is put out of its misery."

Ajaz Ahmed

Building organisational capabilities

MANY YEARS AGO I WAS IN A MOVIE CALLED *Willow*. VAL Kilmer, Warwick Davis and me... and a few thousand other extras. One day we were to fight a huge set-piece battle and I was given (to be honest, quite at random) a fleetingly starring role. I was to run towards Camera 1, behind which Ron Howard was standing in all his majesty, and kill a fleeing enemy soldier. So, amongst all the drama of thousands of struggling men in strange leather uniforms and slightly tanked-up kiwis on horseback, I pursued my enemy towards Camera 1, Ron Howard and glorious filmic immortality.

Regrettably, just as we reached Camera 1 my opponent was struck down by a passing horseman wielding an enormous rubber mallet. I was left standing directly in front of the camera with a raised sword, a surprised look, and no enemy. I did the only sensible thing and acted a swift but noisy death to get out of the way. As I lay on the ground the great Ron Howard delivered his personal director's notes to me: "No one," he said, "dies of a frickin' heart attack on my set!" With that, my Hollywood dreams were over.

"Hire good people who share your values."

Ajaz Ahmed

That moment has stayed with me ever since. It clearly demonstrated that I did not have the capabilities or talents to be a movie actor. The strange thing is that I often see organisations full of people who are not playing by the rules or who lack the capability or talent to succeed in the company or the culture they are in.

In a previous chapter, I spent a lot of time talking about culture. Creating a great culture can be one of the most satisfying things you do as a business owner. Unfortunately, it's not enough. Your business will improve in equity value only if you can show the outside world how that extraordinary performance culture is harnessed to drive sustainable future profit growth because you can employ, retain and grow the BEST talent in your sector.

Your culture is, of course, intimately linked with your talent. In fact your culture can be driven by your focus on talent. Talent can become your chosen context.

In talking to Ajaz Ahmed, he had some interesting insights into the phenomenon that is WPP, the advertising and PR firm run by Martin Sorrell:

> "Everything they do is about 'talent'. They have 25 years of growth but it's not about advertising, it's about being a great home for developing talent. And Martin personifies that. He's a great coach. He personifies WPP."

It's a great example of a business choosing a context and living it. It's a great example of the point I made right at the start of the book about transcending your product and focussing on assets.

Your human assets, your best people, will always be the ones who are aligned with and excited by the culture and purpose of the business. Keith Abel gives the example that:

> "Our Head of Brand started off on the phones in customer services. Your best people are very much the people who just get it, feel it, know what you stand for and personify what it's all about."

Your powerful culture is also, of course, a magnet for talent. Taking the thoughts of Keith Abel again:

> "I remember once we advertised for someone and decided to stick it on the Oxford and Cambridge University websites and we got so inundated with applications that we only interviewed people who had a First Class degree. We just thought, well, that's a reasonable starting point, and we still ended up with a pile this high. We couldn't afford to pay big money and yet attracted really seriously bright people who had great ideas about how they'd like to see things done. And then all we said to them was 'that sounds fantastic, why don't you do that?'"

In other words, set the context and get out of the way.

Whilst running the risk of stating the obvious, talented people who are aligned with and excited by your vision and your purpose come in all shapes and sizes. In the early days there is a natural tendency to attract people who look a lot like you and there is a risk that this becomes a habit. This is not about political correctness – it's a fact that a diverse and balanced talent base in terms of age, gender and life experience is critical to maximising innovation and success. Keith found, for example, that:

> "Having lots of women involved at the top was incredibly important to our success. Our Head of Finance was female and

the MD was female and she was 23 when she was made MD. It was a very good gender and age balance."

Mediocrity is put out of its misery

Having a great culture is not a one-way street. It is not about you giving your people a fun place to work. It is about you providing an environment in which they can be their best. And demanding that they are. You may recall Roger Philby explaining how his amazing culture comes with balancing expectations of staff:

"There's a reason for our culture… we have a nutritionist, we have an amazing culture, we have an amazing intent… we take you on trips abroad, we do all of this really cool stuff. However, by 7.30am this office is buzzing. I can log in at any time of night and I will see my colleagues working, quite literally any time, and if you ever don't pick up your phone, even on a Sunday afternoon and it's your client or your colleague, we will fire you."

Reed Hastings of Netflix invests heavily and courageously in giving his people purpose and autonomy but expects much in return. "Adequate performance," he says, "receives a generous severance package."

To maximise value, therefore, having a great culture where people want to come to work must go hand-in-hand with having the most *talented* people. Essentially this means having the right number of people doing the right jobs with the right level of skills.

You can see the aggregation of all this talent as the *capability* of your business to deliver its plan for future profit growth. This capability must be measured, tracked and developed as an asset in the business.

So, first-off, what is talent and how can we find and foster it?

The Alchemist's view

In conversation with Roger Philby

Roger, Chemistry says its job is to create opportunities for people to be brilliant at work. You help organisations uncover, develop and nurture talent. In the context of an asset what exactly is talent?

"Talent is merely the right person in the right company. The problem with talent is that it implies that someone's special. And I believe everyone's special. I genuinely believe that every human being walking the planet is talent.

"McKinsey produced a book called *The War For Talent* which says there's this talent shortage of 40m people by 2020 and I look at that and go 'There's a talent shortage if you believe talent only looks like X.' In the US there's a leadership talent shortage because the MBA schools in the US cannot turn out enough leaders. That's balls. There's a talent shortage only because you choose to believe that 99.9% of the population can't be great leaders.

"We believe the world is measuring talent wrong by putting all their emphasis on academic ability and experience and neither of these two things in our measurement in the last nine years are ever the most important predictors of performance. I don't care what you've done before and I don't care which school you went to. All I care is, could you be brilliant here?"

If academic ability and experience don't predict talent and performance what does?

"We don't mind sharing any of our IP on the basis that if someone goes out and makes someone else brilliant by stealing our IP, our intent is fulfilled. And so here's our model of talent. Think about five boxes and they're stacked vertically. In the top box put the word Intellect, in the second box down put Values, in the third box Motivation, the fourth Behaviour and in the last put Experience.

So we now have five boxes – Intellect, Values, Motivation, Behaviour and Experience. That's our model of human performance – of talent.

Intellect sits at the top then. Which is measured how?

"The speed at which they take in and retain and process information."

If I'm running a business and I want to build it to, say, £10m and I know asset is the journey and the foundations are my people, how am I supposed to measure intelligence?

"The first thing I would say is define what good looks like. I would take the high performance people I already have and get them to take a Saville Aptitude Test. Then test a bunch of people who don't operate the way you need them to and see if there's a difference. Or have a look at the test norm groups. There are all sorts of norm groups – graduates norm groups, middle manager norm groups, etc. So you can absolutely get a sense of intellect relative to need. Because the point about intellect is trying to determine how much you need. What we frequently find with organisations is they just want bright people. And we're like 'Really, why?' It's about getting really clear what good looks like. What is it about the job that requires a high degree of intellectual horsepower?

"Let me give you an example. If you have an organisation that has sales people in it and you want to move from a product sale to a procurement team, to a solutions sell to a CEO, we would argue one of the step changes you need to make is an increase in the intellectual horsepower of your sales people. Why? (1) products are simpler than solutions so there's a complexity issue; and (2) you shouldn't think about the intelligence of the sales person, you have to think about the intelligence of the customer. And you've just shifted from a middle management person to the CEO and therefore intellect becomes really important.

"Now the reason intellect is at the top of the stack is not because it's the most important but because it's the hardest to change. I cannot make you smarter. I cannot make you process numerical data faster. I can't do that. In the time I have with you I cannot rewire you."

So your five boxes progressively get easier to achieve?

"Yes, exactly."

The second hardest one is therefore Values. Do values include intention or is that a different thing?

"Oh, that's a great question. Let me explain what values do and you might have to help me out with the intention. Values for us are the innate drivers for your behaviour, so things like 'how I value relationships and people' drives a behaviour and 'how I value decision making', whether it's fast and independent or whether it's slow and collaborative."

And in your world, are these subjective or are they objective things?

"Objective, I can measure them."

You measure them, but in the normal business they could make a subjective sniff test?

"Yes, and they do. The challenge with values is that people hire based on their own and the problem with the business that goes from £1m to £10m is that that's ok for the first million, it might even be ok for the second million, by the third and the fourth million the founders and leaders of that are no longer making those decisions.

Someone is putting their own values now on that process so take that up, ratchet that up to a multi-million pound corporation that we work with and what they've got is people who are being hired based on the values of that hiring manager and what they think is right, not what the organisation needs or believes."

This means any successful scalable organisation has to find some objectivity in its values? Values have to be defined, agreed, shared and rooted in an agreed intent?

"Yes, absolutely."

I get Intellect and Values. What comes next? Tell me about Motivations.

"So, values are hard to change – think about your children. If you've got children over the age of eight or nine years old, think about how they value relationships, how they value emotion, how they value conformity, how they value existing systems and processes versus challenging the status quo and doing things differently. I'm not talking about their behaviour but how they feel about it. That is set from the age of eight."

It's hardwired through what they've experienced.

"Exactly, what I'm saying is that when you interview that 30-year-old there's none of that you can change so you'd better bloody well understand whether it's important for your job or not. If you value conformity, if you are FSA regulated or you're a factory and you want someone to stick to an existing process they better not have low conformity, low detail and be motivated by action because they will get you in trouble with the regulator. I could draw the profile of someone from a values, motivations and intellect perspective that will get you in trouble.

"So the challenge to your £1m to £10m company is that at £1m it works ok because you're seeing everyone, the people who have got the values and culture imbedded in them are seeing everyone. What happens when you're a hundred people? So create a process that selects against intellect, values, motivation. And let your hiring managers select against experience but only with people who've got the right intellect, values and motivation.

"So, start building a picture; I'm a £1m organisation going to £10m; this is high growth so this is ambiguous; it's complex; I need people to do multi different roles. What are the values and the motivations of the people who succeed in that environment versus another? If you're a telecoms start-up and you're lured by the fact that someone at BT wants to come to you and you're going to give him equity and they're a big guy and they've got all this experience, test their values and motivations. Be crystal clear what good looks like and not blinded by the fact that he was the number one systems engineer at BT. It isn't going to make him successful in your organisation."

How does this impact on Behaviours?

"Behaviours are interesting because they're all developable. Unlike intellect and values and motivation, it's developable. So the truth is if I behave like my intellect and my values and my motivations all day, none of these people would be working here now. This place would be total anarchy 'coz I love anarchy. I thrive in it, I see it as an opportunistic environment for me, but that's not how organisations like ours grow.

"And so what I've learnt to do is change my behaviour; it doesn't change how I feel, I've just learnt to change my behaviour. If I was put in an environment where I couldn't come up with new ideas I would die on the vine which is really interesting because every programme I've ever been on says you're a high potential and I go, yeah, I am, in a certain type of environment I'm great, put me in another environment I'm lousy."

Is there anything else on talent?

"So, the last thing is experience. I'm not saying experience is not important but you can learn it and we're also saying that it's the least reliable predictor. In every job – actuaries, doctors, nurses – the difference between a great one and an ok one is not knowledge. It's the reason why training fundamentally fails as a behaviour change tool because knowledge is not behaviour. I may know what to do, whether I actually do it or not is driven by my values and motivation. And I will drive that in an environment where my values and motivation resonate with the environment and the culture I am in. So my culture's set up for the right type of person. If you come in here and you're *what good looks like* you will fly. If not you'll be a disaster.

"So today we still walk into our clients and say 75% of your hiring is wrong and they say 'How do you know that?' And we say 'What do you use as your primary screening tool for your hiring?' 92% of the FTSE 100 use the CV as the primary screening tool. And I go 'The CV is less than 10% accurate in predicting future performance.' And then they go 'Oh yeah, but we do interviews.' And I go 'Do you know how accurate interviews are in predicting future performance statistically? No more than 15%.'

"Add those things together, let's say you join the two things up you might get 25% accuracy. And they go 'That can't be true. I wouldn't be a successful business without it.' And I go 'Ok, if you can get more than 25% of the people in your business and you can tell me categorically that you would rehire them knowing what you know now, I'll do the first piece of work at a discount.'"

In conversation with Russell Stinson

Russell, you are very clear that your culture is based on giving opportunities for development for all of your 1300 staff. What does that allow you to do?

"It allows us to add on 30% new business very fast and still continue and deliver great service. If you take a look at starting a new contract, it's all about the staff that deliver it. We put in an experienced supervisor who's going in with a team of people that they have handpicked and we're starting a contract right from the start delivering great service.

"But what about the gaps that were left in the contracts that supervisor and that top team have been pulled out of? That's where service levels lapse in our industry. But because we constantly develop our people from cleaner to supervisor to manager, the No. 2 on the previous contract has already been through the supervisor development programme, and is getting their opportunity to step up. They're happy, they're proud. If you're trying to do that with new staff you'll not deliver the level of service. We've got to have the depth of quality people already in our business.

"To achieve that we have to have people wanting to stay in the business. A kitchen porter who's trained, who understands what we're about as a company, is very different from a kitchen porter who's just asked to clean pots and pans and do the floor. If there's a strong motivation for them to progress they'll deliver excellence. That's why talent is essential even in kitchen cleaning. It's about delivering excellence because people want to progress. They want to do well.

"We're very focused on picking up the small detail. We've got a Head of Excellence who takes a look at everything within the business and if it's not right they're asking questions of anybody within the business – why are we doing this? How can we improve that? That doesn't look right. What do we need to do to make that better? Just constantly trying to make sure that the business is getting better even though it's getting bigger."

The empowerment from measuring capability

I said earlier that it is maximising your talent within a performance culture that builds the capability of the organisation and that this can be measured, tracked and developed as an asset in the business.

There are plenty of ways to assess individual talent, such as GMAT (Graduate Management Admission Test) or the Saville tests (www.savilleconsulting.com), mentioned by Roger above. However, you need to develop a measure of the capability of your *whole* organisation to deliver your commercial vision. This then becomes a KPI you can track. If it's a good measure it can be used at company, division, department and individual level.

You can create your own capability scorecard if you are really clear about *what best looks like* and in what specific areas of business. I declare an interest but have always used the Shirlaws Capability Matrix in running my businesses and thousands of businesses all over the world track against this model. The Matrix is a scorecard system, rating each key function in your business (and there are 20) across five levels of capability, giving a possible total score of 100. It's a great KPI to track and it obviously immediately shows you where the capability gaps are in your business.

The power of the Shirlaws Matrix is that it relates the organisational capability score to the red, blue and black roles in your organisation (you will remember we covered the *red, blue and black* system in Chapter 3).

You'll recall that *red* functions are those that support the business (finance, HR, IT, etc.), *Blue* functions generate cash (sales, marketing, production) and *black* functions are strategic, so essentially grow equity. By bundling the functions of your organisation in this way you can calculate a capability score for the entire back office support (red) area, the whole revenue or operations (blue) area and for the strategic management (black) area. This will tell you a lot about where the capability gaps in your business lie.

As an example, we recently helped a business with these capability calculations. Their back office (red) capability score was more than 80% and their capability score in the black, strategic area was more than 50%. But their capability score in the blue, revenue area was less than 25%. They had invested heavily in systems and ran a very tight ship. Their leadership team was pretty good and had created a certain amount of strategic thinking time. Their revenue-generating functions were very patchy and the business was consequently constantly short of cash. This simple tool helped focus the whole organisation on where it needed to act. The CEO commented:

> "It's been completely empowering to be able to identify our capability gap. We knew something was wrong, but we couldn't pinpoint the problem exactly."

Earlier on I described my own experience of inheriting a strong culture as CEO. So, what of talent and capability? Clearly talent is a crucial element of product delivery in an organisation such as ours. We have a global reputation for entrepreneurial expertise and, to protect that, we generally only accept people to our delivery team who have experience as a CEO in their own right. We need top business people. We also need them free of ego – there is nothing more irritating for the successful entrepreneurs with whom we work than to have some know-it-all telling them how to run their business.

The challenge of recruitment is therefore tremendous. We need to interview dozens of candidates to find the right match. Each of these prospects, quite reasonably, expects to meet the CEO of the organisation she or he is considering joining. To be at all efficient we had to devise a system to *touch* the maximum number of potential recruits, provide them with full information whilst using the minimum capacity of the CEO and leadership team. That system now handles several hundred candidates a year in order to fill the handful of places we offer each year to new coaches and it runs independently of the CEO and senior team.

The key point is that there is a *system*; a documented process that is self-sustaining from a leadership perspective and that can be shown to be an asset to the business. Similarly with capability. Even though our team may have run exceptional businesses themselves, I still felt it was important that we introduced a system of formal certification as a demonstrable asset of capability in the business. That means that all our people have their capabilities measured.

Keeping score

What these examples demonstrate is that for talent and capability to be true assets in the business it is usually necessary to have built measurable and sustainable systems which can be run quite independently of the leadership team.

For the system of measurement to deliver value, it is obviously critical to know what you are measuring and to ensure that, however you design your scorecard, it includes all of the important functions for the role (or if you are assessing the business as a whole, for the organisation).

To be really useful your capability scorecard should score each function against levels of implementation. Just knowing something is very different from having an effective strategy and fully implementing it. But it's useful to measure each of these to see where your strengths and gaps lie. It's useful to know, for example, that your organisation is strong in theoretical knowledge but not good at turning that into fully thought-through strategy. That might explain why great ideas never seem to gain traction and hit the bottom line, or that you implement strategies but then don't sustain them in the mid to long term. That's because the next phase of management capability is lacking.

You also need to be clear what you are measuring best against. Somewhat unconventionally, I think the answer should be *nobody*. This exercise works best if it is *relative to self*. If you were sitting with Usain Bolt and you asked him to compare himself with every other sprinter around the world, how would he rate himself? He would more than likely score close to 100% on a capability analysis scorecard. Every skill would be mastered at depth. And how useful would that exercise be to helping him improve his race? He clearly needs to complete these exercises *relative to himself*. In order words, compared to the level of achievement he wants to create.

By assessing your capability against the goal you have set you will quickly see where your current gaps lie. Your capability scorecard can also evolve as your business grows. You can even reset the context you are scoring yourself in.

For example, to go back to an example Roger used above, you might score very highly if the *self* you are scoring relative to is your £1m business. But how do you score against your £10m self? It's a way of predicting the capabilities you will need going forward. If you like, you can also reset the measure of self against the business you ran a year or two ago. You might be amazed how far your team has already come and that might be a good reason for your Head of Amazing to organise a party.

The Alchemist's view

In conversation with Ajaz Ahmed

Ajaz, what differentiates AKQA? What are you the best in the world at?

"We deliver. That is the ultimate source of scale. The thing I get proudest of is when our work produces exactly the result it is supposed to produce. If you eat the fruit from our farm, I'd be proudest if you said it was the best and tastiest fruit you'd ever tasted. It's irrelevant how big the farm is – I'd rather have a smaller farm producing the best stuff.

"What drives that is the people. The talent. I just hire the best people. If I come across a great person I will hire them even if I have no job for them. In a couple of weeks they'll be adding value, have found their niche and be amazing."

In conversation with Frank Bastow

Frank, you're a small family building firm winning all these awards like the Considerate Constructors Award up against the big boys. You've said a lot of that was down to your culture and ability to grow talent. How do you assess capability in the company?

"We can measure it on our management side. We measure our management in each department on whether they have an awareness of the Shirlaws models. Level one being the understanding, level two is the strategy in our business, and level three is the implementation. Then we calculate that if it's been implemented all the way through the business, we take that as level four. Level five is where the methodology is so effective that we leverage it in other areas of our business.

You literally use the Shirlaws Capability Matrix to assess your management team?

"Yes. To be honest we haven't done that for a year. I would like to revisit, especially now we've got the new Managing Director. Last time we scored 78."

What were you when you first completed the Matrix?

"We were 23 and, I tell you what, I knew it was 23 as well! I knew there were these big gaps but our management team didn't know, so we couldn't develop any further down, get any real depth. We had a lot of knowledge but hadn't written anything down. That was the whole point, it was all in people's heads.

"So as soon as we did the Bastow Bible, we covered all our Level 2 which meant writing down a strategy in each area and that made it possible to really implement the important stuff. So once we had it written down that's what got us up to a 78. And a lot of that we then managed to drive all the way through to the factory floor."

Action plan: 10 things in 100 days

1. Develop a real **focus on your culture**, particularly if you have taken the eye of this particular ball in the last few difficult years. Think of inspiring but implementable ways to create a transformational culture; allocate a generous budget. Should you appoint a Head of Amazing?

2. Ensure your culture is based on the three principles of **purpose**, **autonomy** and **mastery**. Are you setting the context? Do you have the courage and confidence to genuinely give your people autonomy? Is yours really a learning culture in which your people grow and develop every day? If not, now is the time to do something about it. A culture is not expensive to create. It just takes time and commitment.

3. Set aside one of your quarterly retreats for culture. Take your key team offsite to **uncover and agree the intent in your business**. What purpose do you serve? Are you inspiring and rallying your people and their passions around that purpose? Ensure it is something that you and your team can take pride in. Try to find some emotive language that will engage your people at a deeper level. External facilitation is a great idea.

4. Unless you have recently conducted **a full and proper values exercise** that you are proud of, do one this quarter. Appoint a Champion to run it for you but you MUST be actively involved as sponsor. Have your Champion run a workshop or series of workshops so that everyone has the chance to contribute. Ensure you define what your values mean and attribute measurable behaviours.

5. Choose to **focus on your leadership style**. Leadership is about confidence, vision and inspiration. The source of all this is an understanding of your own intent and purpose. Find it! In other words, make sure you are very clear of your context. Manage the energy of your team every day. Collaborate but have the confidence to trust your instincts and ensure you are decisive and clear. Consider coaching if you feel it will help you.

6. **Improve your communication abilities**. What is the *Nelson Touch* to you? Consider adopting 10 Things in 100 Days or another way to improve communication in your business. Communicate regularly and honestly with your team. Consider a daily or at least a weekly blog. If your people are at multiple sites, use technology. I have found PresentMe (**www.presentme.com**) to be a great tool for creating engaging communication of factual information.

7. **Take a good look at your talent**. Define very clearly *what good looks like*. Work out how to measure that. Agree the values and motivations that are important in the talent you seek to hire.

8. Think about what learning, skill transfer and coaching means in your organisation. **Create a strategy for continual development of the whole team**. Remember that the most motivated people are those that feel they are challenged and constantly developing *mastery*.

9. Start to **definitively measure the capability of your organisation**. Create a capability scorecard of some sort so that you can measure capability at an individual and organisational level. Measure progress *relative to self*. Use this measure to plot progress, which will generate energy and confidence for yourself and the team.

10. Start to **systemise your culture, talent and capability** as much as possible. At every opportunity put in place documented systems and written policies for culture, recruitment, talent management, capability, etc. Pass this skill on to the next level of management so that you can move on, leaving a replicable system in place.

Chapter 7.
A Smith & Wesson Trumps Four Aces*

*The title of this chapter is a quote from *Velocity*, by Ajaz Ahmed and Stefan Olander.

"We cannot solve a problem by using the same kind of thinking we used when we created it."

Albert Einstein

A culture of innovation

V+7	Scale
V+6	Brand architecture
V+5	Channel extension
V+4	Product extension
(V+3)	Systems / product innovation
V+2	Talent / capability / culture
VI	————————————— Industry benchmark

I T FEELS LIKE WE HAVE COVERED A LOT — GETTING A BRILLIANT platform in place, understanding where your business is in the cycle, and building a brilliant performance culture full of aligned talent and capability. Yet these are just the foundations. The real asset-build starts here.

The previous three chapters were all about building and leading a great culture, but what is the purpose of that culture? What is it for?

The obvious answer, in the context of building assets, is that it creates the potential for the future reliable growth of wealth-generative assets in the business. A truly self-responsible and aligned culture creates the opportunity for the business to innovate. It also frees you and your leadership team from the day-to-day operations of the business so that you can lead this innovation.

If at the word *innovation* your heart sank, you are not alone. We are constantly told by consultants and pundits to innovate in our businesses. There are hundreds of books on the subject of innovation. And yet most entrepreneurs, as eloquently described by Keith Abel, find focusing on what we do really well, rather than constantly reinventing stuff, is usually the key to success. How should we resolve this apparent dilemma?

The truth is that both are right. Businesses need to innovate – but only after taking a visceral understanding of what they are really good at as a starting point.

In my world, *innovation* just means doing things differently. It doesn't have to be rocket science. It doesn't have to be radical. It can be an iterative process of getting everything in the business better and better. What Nick Jenkins of Moonpig.com called "constant polishing" of what you do and how the customer experiences it.

"Your biggest opportunity may be right where you are now."

Napoleon Hill

Similarly, I was struck by Rupert Lee-Browne's response to my question of what was the unique formula that built his business to the scale it is at today. "We don't really have one," he said, "except for the fact that every day we're going to do it slightly better than everyone else."

However, whilst a lot of innovation is iterative and involves *polishing*, every business should also explore where the big opportunities lie. This can be fairly stretching.

The problem is that most of us are not terribly good at looking at things in a completely different way. In Donald Rumsfeld's immortal words, we are not good at identifying the "unknown unknowns... the things we don't know we don't know." We are effectively programmed to make our future decisions by looking back on what we have already experienced. We are good at identifying patterns and following those blueprints to guide our decision-making. Great if you are hunting an aurochs, but not brilliant if you want to make a major creative leap.

As Roger von Oech commented:

> "It's easy to come up with new ideas; the hard part is letting go of what worked for you two years ago, but will soon be out of date."

Continuing this theme, in their tremendous book *Velocity*, from which I borrowed the title of this chapter, Ajaz Ahmed and Stefan Olander make the point that:

> "Rarely is there an inclination to mess with a winning formula until it's too late. You have to innovate product constantly. And keep working at it. A sense of entitlement is the enemy of innovation."

Breaking the pattern

For these big innovations it's therefore important to *get out of the pattern* and free your mind to see the real opportunities. There are lots of ways to do this, some of which I list below, and some more of which you can find in the range of great books on the subject.

A good starting point is to look as widely as possible and as contextually as possible for the major trends – not just in your sector but globally –

to see what opportunities there are for you. There are lots of resources to help with this, from futurology talks online to TED talks (**www.ted.com**). If you are in the UK, the organisation Benchmark for Business (**www.benchmarkforbusiness.com**) puts on some exceptionally stimulating days of insight, delivered by global business figures. The point is to train yourself out of your existing patterns and look outward to the world, not just inward on your own business.

I sometimes do a Google search on "megatrends" and this is usually quite fun. As I search at the time of writing, the internet tells me the megatrends include demographic shift (aging population, the passing of the peak child point, etc.), economic shifts, urbanisation, resource scarcity and technology (including nanotechnology). None of these are in any sense new or surprising but getting into the detail of them might spark an idea for how innovation can capture future opportunities for your business.

The point is that *doing things differently* has to be (or become) central to how you run your business if you seriously want to grow assets. It must not be something that other businesses do. Businesses that don't innovate are P&L-driven, they are not asset-led businesses. Leadership teams who don't drive innovation are operators and not builders.

Ajaz Ahmed makes the point that:

> "Innovation has to be a constant state of mind. You have to embrace innovation as part of the DNA. You have to institutionalise innovation."

My belief is that innovation is becoming more and more important against a background of accelerating change and broader willingness in most cultures to experiment. I also recognise that it has never been easier to get new ideas in front of a global audience through multiple channels.

At the time of writing there is one more factor. We are on the cusp of, I believe, a significant and sustained recovery in the global economic cycle. After profound recessions, all the evidence suggests that consumers, both businesses and individuals, look for new ideas as they start to buy again, rather than necessarily buying the solutions they were used to prior to the downturn.

Marketing literature is full of examples of innovative brands emerging at this point in the cycle. Businesses that do not innovate tend to get left behind at an accelerated rate in this recovery phase, which gives an added incentive to all businesses to innovate NOW.

Those who run smaller entrepreneurial businesses are fortunate in this respect. A smaller business is far more agile than a large corporate organisation. If it chooses to, a small or medium business can change fast.

Execution, not inspiration

A critical point to bear in mind is that innovation is not about *having ideas*. It is about implementing ideas. Innovation is about execution and not just inspiration.

> *"Innovation is the ability to convert ideas into invoices."*
>
> **L. Duncan**

So, from a practical perspective, how do you go about innovating and what should you innovate to create the greatest asset uplift?

Firstly, and rather obviously, you need to have the time, focus and resources to devote to new thinking. Practically, this means you must be *above benchmark* with your business platform in place and you must have the culture to support it.

You also need to have the energetic focus and passion to look for opportunities (big and small) and then design and execute solutions. That means you need to *be at the right point on the Stages cycle* (Chapter 2). It's fine if you are feeling relaxed and confident early in your growth phase but if you are stressed, or worse disillusioned, you are not in the right place to innovate. You need to focus on the five key skills we explored (also in Chapter 2) to re-energise yourself and your business.

Then you need to *get your team around you*. Innovation is a team sport. When doing this myself I have put together small teams to focus on particular aspects of the business and have these meet regularly. Innovation might be all they do, but in most cases you are just carving out some focused time as part of their day job.

You may recall Keith Abel's description of how he galvanised his team behind innovations to save Abel & Cole:

> "We invited everyone to come to my house in five groups to discuss what they'd like to do with the business, and we called them different projects. We had Project Shuffle... We had Project Kindness... We had Project Product.

> "And the deal was that Ted and I tried as much as possible to shut up. We said, 'Just come up with five things that you think we could improve on,' in each Project. Then we might have 200 ideas written up on sheets of paper all around the walls.

"Then we broke up into five groups and one would go into the dining room, one would go in here, one would go in the hallway and they would discuss those five things and then they'd come back with what they thought were the very best ideas that were coming out of that day. And you could guarantee that whatever Ted and I thought was the most important idea of the day was always in that group, and on top of it there would be things we would never have thought of. And then we'd say, 'Brilliant guys, that's what we're going to do.' So it was no longer our ideas, it was their ideas, and they'd go back into work and go 'It's brilliant, you know we've been saying we wanted to do that for ages.'"

When doing an exercise like this your team should *include your customers* – if not literally then conceptually. For instance, I heard Annabel Karmel – the wonderful baby nutrition entrepreneur who is largely responsible for me and my wife now having a couple of strapping rugby-playing boys who love food – say that she "spends a lot of time listening to feedback from the mums who use my books and buy my food. I learn so much from them."

In my conversation with Keith I was struck by how, even as CEO of a £50m business, he still mans the inbound order line and talks to customers when he can. Wherever possible I think it's critical for you and your whole team to be a customer of your own service or product and regularly experience it at first hand. That will be a powerful trigger for constant innovation.

I think it helps to come up with a *problem statement* to define what specifically you are trying to solve. This might be small and iterative or it might be game-changing, depending on what your business needs at the time. Make this real. Ideally make it a necessity. If it's not a real driving need in the business your brain and those around you won't strive to solve it.

One way to do this is to make a bold declaration of intent to inspire your team to excel. And link this to the driving needs of the organisation. John F. Kennedy's famous statement of 25 May 1961 that "the United States should set as a goal the landing of a man on the moon and returning him safely to the earth by the end of the decade" is a celebrated example of a declaration of intent. What is forgotten is that this declaration was made as a Special Message to Congress on Urgent National Needs – intent was being linked to need. Ajaz Ahmed concurs when he says: "You need to start with a rule – a statement of intent – and the leaders must lead by example."

Language is important here. A statement of intent based on "Let's go and get..." is a lot more attractive, and likely to generate more creativity, than "We need to get...".

One useful rule of thumb is that if you want to really get somewhere then give your brain a bigger problem. As a simple example, rather than think, "We are at £8m, how do we get to £10m?" think, "What would we do to get to £100m?" It is not about the practicality of the goal but the stimulation to creativity of opening space and creating a more extreme choice. *Think big in innovation.*

Ideally, innovation should be in something you love doing. Make it fun. Innovation literature is full of ideas on how to engage your creative brain and these are worth exploring if you are running an innovation session. *The Lean Startup: How Constant Innovation Creates Radically Successful Businesses* by Eric Ries is a classic, as is *The Ten Faces of Innovation: Strategies for Heightening Creativity* by Tom Kelley. I also recommend *Business Model Generation: A Handbook for Visionaries, Game Changers, and Challengers* by Alexander Osterwalder and Yves Pigneur.

Innovation should, however, be a state of mind and not just confined to a wacky session, so you will need to find ways of making the generation of ideas rewarding and fun on a day-to-day basis.

Try not to obsessively focus on only one aspect. Innovation is a set of ingredients. If you are thinking big then also think wide. To quote Larry Keeley in *Ten Types of Innovation*:

> "The most certain way to fail is to focus only on one product. Successful innovators use many types of innovation."

Base your innovation on as much analysis and data as you can. Know your business drivers. Know your market. Know your customers. Use that knowledge and any data you can to drive change.

Look for ideas widely and not just in your business or in your sector. How have other people taken a bold step to do something better and how can you learn from them? Keep your antennae up all the time.

I try to look at ideas in context (returning to a theme of Chapter 5). If I see something that impresses me as innovative I'll try not to concentrate on the product itself (the *content*) but look for the one word that sits at the source of the idea and then apply that word or idea to elements of my own business and see what pops up. Usually nothing will result, but on a rare occasion it's a simple way to a new line of thinking.

Make innovation, or doing things differently, part of the everyday culture of your business. Practice the principles and process of innovation so that when the really *big idea* comes along you recognise it and are ready to act.

Finally, persevere. James Dyson is said to have had 5126 failed prototypes before number 5127 worked and became the basis on which £800m of annual sales have subsequently been built. To allow for that perseverance you'd better make it fun and rewarding for yourself and for the whole team to be innovative. Take another look at that *culture layer* and make sure it's fun to innovate.

That is a lot of information, so here is a quick summary of my top ten tips for executing innovation:

1. Be above benchmark and at the right point on the Stages cycle.

2. Get your team around you.

3. Include your customers.

4. Make a bold declaration of intent.

5. Give your brain a bigger problem.

6. Don't focus on only one aspect.

7. Base your innovation on as much analysis and data as you can.

8. Look for ideas widely.

9. Make innovation part of the everyday culture and make it fun.

10. Persevere.

Incidentally, I also think it's a good idea to have someone who is responsible for innovation in the business. I don't mean an *innovations centre* as this risks becoming an ivory tower; I firmly believe that everyone should be involved in your innovation culture.

What I mean is that there can be someone who is responsible for innovation, who inspires and facilitates it. You may recall Roger Philby's Head of Amazing. This is all about creating an amazing place to work and the idea can be stretched only slightly to be about creating a place where everyone has amazing ideas.

What we are talking about creating here is a unique bank of knowledge in your business both in terms of the outcome (new stuff) but also the process of how you got there. It is really important to document all of this to make it replicable and so that it builds up into a demonstrable asset.

Where to innovate

All very insightful perhaps but what precisely should you be innovating? What should you be doing differently?

This is obviously your choice. However, one way to get a grip on this is to break the rather overwhelming task up contextually. Remember the system of red, blue and black covered in Chapter 3? As a reminder, red stuff is all of the infrastructure in the business, blue stuff makes you money today (sales and factory, etc.), and black stuff is all about strategy and leveraging your assets to create equity build (position, IP, M&A, etc.). You might use a simple tool like this to see where you can innovate and to prioritise.

You might list all the functions of your business in three columns (a red one, a blue one and a black one) and start to analyse where innovation would give you the biggest return. For example, in your red column you list everything in your cost management system including finance, IT, the management of people, legal, premises, etc.

In your blue column you list everything in your revenue system and everything about your product including product design, factory, sales, delivery, etc. These are big catch-all (contextual) titles and you may well need to drill down into the content in each of these as it is relevant in your business. You may come up with quite a big list.

Then you might run a problem statement over this list and see which areas stand out as likely to deliver a return against that problem statement. Ideally you should think of that return in equity terms rather than just profit. Don't lose sight of the fact that equity can be both cultural and commercial. An innovation that makes your people – or you – happier, more fulfilled and more productive can be just as valuable in equity terms as one that drives revenue or more immediate *value*.

The useful thing about using a tool like this that is based on the functions of the business rather than outputs is that it should be pretty clear who is responsible for driving the innovation project once you have decided your priorities. If you have built your functional platform to benchmark, you will have clear responsibilities for each area of the business and there will be a genuinely empowered and self-responsible person for each. That person can then easily and seamlessly pick up the project with his or her team. If you find you don't have that level of responsibility you might revisit your platform at this point.

However you identify them, in most businesses I have seen innovations turn up in three main chunks: systems, products and growth. By growth I mean innovations that are really game-changing for the business. I'll cover these in the next four chapters.

For now, let's take a look at the first two in the list – systems and products.

Systems innovation

Ajaz Ahmed is clear that when it comes to innovation, focusing on the systems in your business is absolutely critical.

"Innovation isn't just about the product. You have to improve every aspect of the business. At AKQA we are obsessed with systems and innovating our system to be better. You should systemise what you can and use human beings to add creativity.

"If you get the system right it allows you to scale... it gives people the freedom to create growth. The ideal business is the one that can balance great systems and operational excellence with creativity and experimentation. It's no surprise that Tim Cook,

CEO of Apple, had a background in systems before he joined Apple. Today, Apple's systems work best. They are the best in the world at it."

The business system is obviously *how you do what you do* and includes all the elements of your business platform.

Innovation can be radical here. It might be buying in a whole new system of technology, communications or production. It might be buying another business for their system.

However, it is often simply a matter of iterative steps of constant improvement. To quote Nick Jenkins, whose Moonpig.com system is somewhat legendary:

> "It took us probably two years to get the system right. Our business was driven entirely by data, we were constantly collecting data on what our customers were doing when they visited the site, when they bought and when they came back. We would churn that data again and again to work out exactly what our customers were doing. We used that data to polish the site – looking at how customers arrive, leave and behave on site.

> "There's a path through the website and you'll find certain sticking points and that could be the language, could be the buttons, so you just keep polishing and polishing and polishing that until you get more people coming out at the other end. We would, for example, measure the performance of a particular card so we would look at all the data that we had for all sessions and we would look at the number of times a card had been looked at versus the number of times it had ever got bought and work out whether or not that was a successful card. Not how many times it had sold but how many times it got looked at versus how many times it sold."

What I heard in this part of our conversation was a combination of a number of the themes covered above: understanding the numbers and how to analyse these, *listening* to the customer and constantly innovating by polishing the delivery system. Nick goes on to explain the system in more detail:

> "We always had a razor-like focus on what we needed to understand about the business to understand if it was working. The critical thing was being able to model what customers were going to do over the next two years. We developed a spreadsheet which was fine-tuned over the years so as we got more and more data we put more and more in, it was a model, a sales model, into which we would enter how much money we were going to spend on advertising, what the expected cost of customer acquisition was going to be, what the spending pattern of that customer was in the first year, what the referral pattern of that customer would be in the first year and all of this would be built in with seasonal adjustments for different times of the year.

> "And we were projecting accurately 12 months forward, plus or minus 5% what we were going to do. We always had a really, really good understanding of how our customers would behave which is easy to do when you've got hundreds of thousands of customers, which we did when we started measuring it, and millions of course at the end."

Clearly the Moonpig.com system had enormous value to the business; it effectively drove profit growth and was a key part of the platform that allowed the business to scale to millions of customers. It therefore became an asset in its own right as it drove future cash flow. But was it also an *asset* because it could be worth more to another business? That is to say, is the system a structure or process that could be slotted into other businesses to improve their operations?

I think this is where innovation and systems become really interesting. Of course we develop and fine-tune our systems to reduce cost and facilitate revenue growth. But there is a point at which your system becomes an asset both because it is the basis of your future growth and possibly because it is worth even more to someone else than it is to you. It is really worthwhile to take a good look at your systems through this asset lens and see what opportunities this might reveal and what changes and innovations this might inspire.

Attentive readers, or possibly those interested in climbing, may recall that right at the beginning of the book I said that I had learnt a lot about siege climbing on Aconcagua. The purpose in mentioning it once again here is that it demonstrates the use of a system to manage an otherwise impossible task. The system I observed involved establishing a line of camps up the mountain that we stocked with food, water and fuel by repeatedly ascending and descending between camps, gradually building the *platform* from which the final assault could be launched and the climbers recovered. We also needed to establish fixed ropes and other technical stuff. The system allowed us to achieve the goal.

A business I know well recently had a professional valuation performed. This business has developed a superb system to manage the people and processes with the intention to reduce cost. However, the outcome has been the creation of an asset which was valued at £1.3m in its own right.

The system has become part of the IP of the business. It creates value because it allows for other assets to be developed. Seeing your system in this way can be transformational – like the insurance broking business that realised its IP was not really insurance but its cutting-edge telemarketing system (developed to drive P&L). That insight allowed the business to create radical, high-value product extensions that had nothing to do with insurance.

The story of the acquisition of the Kiddicare brand by the UK supermarket Morrisons for a very bullish multiple is quite well known. Morrisons paid top dollar for Kiddicare not just because it was a great trading business with a good platform, management, etc. The enhanced valuation of the business was based on Kiddicare having an asset that was hugely valuable to Morrisons. Namely, Kiddicare had a fantastic online system that would have taken the acquiring business significant time and treasure to develop itself and effectively this allowed Morrisons to catch up with rivals. The point is that Kiddicare was worth more because of its *system*. The system drove the multiple and not just the profit, significantly increasing the value of the business for its founders.

In 2008 I was asked to advise a global property business on its operations in Eastern Europe. This was a great business facing a number of challenges around its speed of growth and it was these challenges we were asked to work on with the leadership team.

However, what was really interesting to me was the discussion we had around the assets in the business. In order to penetrate this emerging Eastern European market the business had invested in a superb back office system – in other words it had made an investment in its *red*. This allowed the business to manage costs very efficiently and created a platform for revenue growth regionally. The thing about red is that it is highly transferable to other businesses, even in different sectors.

At the time, a lot of inbound investment was going into the region from Western Europe and the US. What these businesses – whether accountants, lawyers or other service businesses – lacked was an effective, local, back-office. Suddenly our property company's back-office system had ceased to be a cost and became an asset. It could be sold to other non-competitive businesses. Their *red* had become *blue*.

From a systems perspective, seeing your back-office cost as an asset is a fairly innovative shift. It requires quite a different pattern of thought. Without fundamentally changing that pattern would that business have seen the opportunity? Probably not.

This demonstrates why innovation requires a fundamental change in how the senior team thinks about their business. In this case, it also demonstrates powerfully the benefits of bringing in external advice and challenge to your business. If you need to fundamentally change the pattern then *do it yourself* may very well not be enough.

The Alchemist's view

In conversation with Ajaz Ahmed

Ajaz, at AKQA the first of your values is innovation. Tell me more about that.

"We are obsessed with innovation – by doing something new. It is in our DNA. If your core intention is to create the future you have to do things differently. Yet we don't have a Head of Innovation. Everyone, absolutely everyone, in the organisation is driven by innovation, service, quality and thought."

AKQA is an ideas and innovation company. What advice would you have for entrepreneurs around innovation?

"Start by asking 'What's interesting about your company? What is interesting about your product? What is the magic?'

"Innovation has to be a constant state of mind. You have to embrace innovation as part of the DNA. You have to institutionalise innovation. The trouble is that rarely is there an inclination to mess with a winning formula until it's too late. You have to innovate product constantly. And keep working at it. A sense of entitlement is the enemy of innovation.

"But it isn't just about the product. You have to improve every aspect of the business. At AKQA we are obsessed with systems and innovating our system to be better. My view is that if a machine can do something you should get the machine to do it. Human beings are creative and expressive. You should systemise what you can and use human beings to add value. To add creativity.

"You need to start with a rule – a statement of intent – and the leaders must lead by example. When we went all-digital at AKQA, when we moved to a clutter-free office, that meant everything; all of our financial systems are paperless, all of our suppliers are paperless, we stopped printed magazines from being delivered to us. If you get the system right it allows you to scale the business. A lot of our competitors have stayed the same size but we have grown partly because we had a scalable system.

"The point is that having a system gives people the freedom to create. To create growth. The ideal business is the one that can balance great systems and operational excellence with creativity and experimentation.

"It's no surprise that Tim Cook, CEO of Apple, had a background in inventory management, logistics, distribution, system before he joined Apple. Today, Apple's systems work best. They are the best in the world at it."

In conversation with Rupert Lee-Browne

Rupert, please tell me about systems innovation in your business. I can only imagine it is absolutely central to the success of a business such as yours.

"In terms of basic systems and processes we are kind of already there. We have spent a decade making the customer experience really smooth and efficient. From the customer's perspective it all works seamlessly so if you want to send a hundred pounds to your granny in Guadeloupe you can do that all online, and you can do it at three in the morning if you want. Or if you feel more comfortable speaking to someone on the phone then you can do that too.

"Better still, if you're an SME owner or manager and you want to pay your invoices to your guy in China, or Canada or wherever, you can do that all online at three in the morning, safe in the knowledge that it's going to be there when required and that amazingly the service is free.

"It's behind the scenes that we're working hard to improve and change things so that we can build out a whole new set of services and to make efficiencies in our processes. Technology is at the heart of this and we have been moving our emphasis towards technology, with a view to how we deliver our service in the future. Technology allied with amazing service will determine our growth."

In conversation with Frank Bastow

Frank, you describe how your culture results in creative people asking "I don't know why we do it this way?" How does that innovation add value to your business?

"We make our lives and the customers' lives easier by simplifying stuff."

Your system?

"Yes. For example, you see everybody on building sites now with identity tags, you know? We started that idea. We work in these big residential buildings in London and people get nervous about contractors coming and going. We wanted to take away that anxiety. So we created a system that's all integrated so that a letter goes through every resident's door to say who the site agent is, what his telephone number is, and that automatically creates photo-identity tags and letters. It just made life so much easier. We have a site list of everything our guys need to do to get set-up on site and if you tick those all off, our life is a lot easier. And it even goes down to simple things like making friends with the caretaker.

"If we can take the aggravation away from the surveyor, they will use us again because they had an easy life and made easy money. It's all about making people's lives easier."

And how is that system worth money?

"Because it saves time and effort, aggravation and money. Because it makes people want to use us again."

And do you sell it?

"No. That's the other thing, our costing system as well, we should have sold that a long time ago but it gives us such an advantage. I said, 'Wouldn't it be great if I had an estimating system that did this?' So we wrote a programme over about six months that allocates cost to all our different sub-contractors, so that I can do interim valuations, etc. We could sell that programme and I'm thinking I should do an online version of it. That's what I should do."

So you've got product innovation and systems innovation, both of which save you money and therefore drive your P (profit) but actually they drive your M (multiple) because they free up time, creativity and they are in themselves valuable.

"Yes, and they give us a competitive edge. I think what I've been frightened of is giving it to everybody else. But you should be like a chef, you shouldn't be worried about giving away the ingredients and how you make cakes or how you make a dish, it's the way that you make it that makes it clever."

In conversation with Russell Stinson

Russell, you said earlier that you wanted to build something that has real foundations and to see your business as an asset. Tell me about what innovations you've made in your systems to create that asset.

"So, firstly we need to take a look at quality monitoring. We've got people who are completely independent of operations and they will go in and take a look at every aspect of the cleaning and it's all on a system, it's all scored, on a percentage. Within two hours that report's electronically generated with an action list with photographs that go out to the operations manager to get dealt with within 48 hours. Essentially we're looking to get every site to 100%. From a system point of view, it's completely scalable, no matter how many sites we have.

"And that is true of all of our systems. For example, invoicing and payroll which automatically generate profit per contract so we know that we're achieving our margins across 110 clients as soon as the invoicing and payroll is completed. It's not a manual process.

"If you take a look at the HR aspect, everybody who comes into the company to register logs on at a terminal, goes through a set of questions, then there's an interview that they then go through. If they pass they go through to our pool of staff that are available for work. Our operations managers have all got iPads, they can see all those pool of people that are ready for trial and if they need somebody for a trial they have a ready bank of people who are registered, who have got all their compliance to work, all the papers checked if they are non-EU nationals, who have passed a competency-based interview, understand what we're about as a company, ready to go to a trial. If they pass that trial, the operations managers update that on their iPad and set them up for an induction which they come to do at the office.

That induction is completed, uniforms allocated – all recorded and all of it is done from within a centralised system.

"We're working in an industry where health and safety and where training are absolutely paramount. We have a set of training records, electronically assigned to each site and if you work at that site your payroll record that's put on to the system dynamically links you to your training record so the operations managers know all of the training that they have to have on those sites and we've got a percentage score on a weekly basis where we know each of those sites and their training records.

"It's not paper-based, it's not somebody running around trying to find out how training is within the company, it's managed by the Head of Excellence and is all centrally linked so one record for one employee will have their payroll, their training, the amount of time they've been with us, etc. It allows us to look at staff retention, progression, and links to a capability matrix so that we know where we are with our rising stars as well.

And it makes you entirely scalable.

"We're looking to get to 5000 staff – we're doing that from a very comfortable position where we know the systems are completely scalable."

Very impressive. So your system is an asset because it allows for scale – for future profit growth. In addition to that, is it also an asset in that you could sell it to someone else? Or because it allows you to expand through acquisition on to your scalable platform?

"That's something that we have taken a look at. In my experience no one is operating with anything like our system. We've had officials from the UK Border Agency review our system because they're obviously checking a lot of other companies around how people manage passport checks. Because our processes and systems are all automated, they said there's no company that has got anything like how we manage that process."

Theoretically, you could turn that into a stand-alone company, which means it is a genuine asset in the business.

"Yes. If we chose to."

Your innovation of systems is very impressive. What about product? Product one is cleaning kitchens and hotels... what else?

"Are we looking to just stay in hospitality? This is a live conversation but we need to really understand our core assets – our intellectual property – before we are comfortable with developing into new products and markets. Whatever we do, we will retain our focus – our people, our focus on five-star hospitality, the quality, the relationship, the peace of mind, the systems, the quality monitoring. Those are our assets."

Product innovation

Giving customers extra

"We need to really understand our core assets – our intellectual property – before we are comfortable with developing into new products."

So says Russell Stinson and this opens up a fascinating conversation about product innovation.

Everything we covered above about innovation in systems is equally, if not more, true of product innovation. Getting creative about what customers give you money for – or more importantly *might wish to give* you money for – is critical to the asset growth of the business. Just as I discussed above, a constant quest to polish and improve your product is critical. And the role of the customer as the source of inspiration and ideas is key.

Polishing and improving your product is vital from a revenue perspective. Innovating how you deliver your product is equally vital. It should be a constant task to think innovatively about how to give customers more than they expect – to give them extras that make them feel rewarded, to secure loyalty and, of course, develop noise around your proposition. The innovative element is to keep delivering different kinds of extras and to avoid the mistake of your expensive extra becoming tomorrow's standard with no associated benefit to you and a big impact on your margin.

I enjoyed what WestJet did around Christmas 2013. They mocked up an automatic check-in terminal such that when the passenger scanned their boarding pass Santa appeared on a video link from Lapland and engaged in a personal conversation. Amongst other things Santa slipped in a question about what the passenger wanted for Christmas.

On arrival at their destination what came round the carrousel? Not luggage but beautifully wrapped gifts, personalised for each passenger. While the aircraft was in the air the WestJet team at the destination airport had raced round the local mall buying and wrapping the inevitable socks and scarves but also flat-screen TVs, cameras and snowboards.

To drive real *asset growth* and wealth, innovation of product should involve the creation of distinct new product offerings. Generally speaking your second product is more profitable – sometimes many times more profitable – than your first. This is, rather obviously, because the costs of bringing the product to market, including the costs of acquisition of clients, are generally largely covered by your first product (P1).

On the P side of the equation this clearly drives additional profit for the second product. But it *also* drives the M side because the demonstrable ability to develop and successfully launch additional products creates a valuable asset in the business, which has a quantifiable value. A buyer or investor will see this as a sign of incremental future revenue growth and value the asset accordingly. It may also be a skill the buyer or investing partner might value in their own business.

Rather like systems innovation, therefore, product innovation is a *double whammy* – piling on higher margin revenue whilst simultaneously enhancing the multiple.

Don't be frozen out by corporate myopia

Product innovation is also the only way to protect against the market moving on and leaving you behind as it is increasingly wont to do in this fast-moving age of quick-to-market disruptive technologies and, arguably, in the immediate growth spurt post-recession.

I find the story of the US ice trade fascinating. Really. Did you know that in the middle of the 19th century the harvesting of ice from North American lakes employed 90,000 people and was capitalised at nearly $1bn in today's money? Companies like The Wenham Lake Ice Company, which we met briefly in Chapter 3, were global brands exporting to Europe, India and China.

Yet the business died almost overnight as industrial refrigeration was developed. And was it Wenham that invested their considerable profits in driving this innovation? Of course not. Their thinking pattern would not let them see the coming seismic shift. As we covered in Chapter 3, the external factors destroyed the value in the business and, in a story repeated down the ages, the management team was too inwardly-focused and unresponsive to see it coming. They discounted the disruptive technology as irrelevant, expensive and unreliable. And paid the consequences.

Here are some more examples of this corporate myopia:

"Who the hell wants to hear actors talk?"

Harry M. Warner, Warner Bros Pictures, 1927

"The horse is here today, but the automobile is only a novelty – a fad."

President of Michigan Savings Bank investment advice on the Ford Motor Company

"What use could the company make of an electric toy?"

Western Union, when it turned down rights to the telephone in 1878

We can all have a laugh at this apparent stupidity but then we must ask ourselves how much knowledge do we really have of what will be impacting our industries in five or ten years? How much do we really know what is happening in Brazil, Indonesia or Hong Kong where innovation is a constant? That's why it is so critical to be looking out and not in and keeping our antennae up for what is really going on in our sector and more broadly in the world. That is why it is so critical to be innovating new products and making innovation of product a habit.

It's therefore somewhat perplexing how many otherwise great businesses develop a blind spot around product innovation. So many businesses cling tenaciously to their initial product (lake ice) – perhaps because it was why they started the business in the first place – but fail to really innovate.

If this seems an unfair criticism, I should probably explain what I mean by *product*. To me it is what the customer cheerfully parts with their cash in exchange for. It is the foundation piece of the business. I often have this debate with lawyers, for example, who will say "We have lots of products; commercial law, property law, family law." My view is that these are all one product. I give my money to my lawyer for legal advice and that is the product. Now, if they leveraged their assets to give me additional business advice outside of the law, for example, that would be a new product. That would be innovation.

Of course, this runs the risk of becoming rather semantic. Is it a new product (P2) or just an iteration of the existing product (P1)? In many ways, I don't think it matters so long as you are asking the questions. The definitions are up to you.

To go back to what Russell said above, the critical thing is that the business innovates, and innovates from a real understanding of its core assets or core value proposition. It's absolutely critical to understand your core IP and to ask yourself "Are we *really* innovating? And, given these assets, what might customers give us money for?"

Inevitably, the best examples of product innovation come from the corporate world and the brands we all know so well. It's of limited value to rehash the well-known stories of Apple or Gillette but it is worth looking at these businesses closely and comparing them to what you do in your own. I think a good business to look at just at the moment is Amazon. Consider how it evolved from being a retailer of books ("earth's biggest bookstore") and has constantly innovated against its core assets of simplicity of delivery into multiple products and now devices.

And if it's tempting to say, "It's easy for them with their huge resources" it may be worth revisiting those words of Steve Jobs:

> "Innovation has nothing to do with how many R&D dollars you have. It's not about money. It's about the people you have, how they're led, and how much you get it."

In other words it's about you and your attitude.

The Alchemist's view

In conversation with Keith Abel

Keith, tell me about innovation in a business that started delivering bags of potatoes and now has around 500 SKUs generating north of £50m per year.

"Well, I started the business knocking on people's doors with potatoes. That was new. That little innovation is now responsible for around £8m of our sales. And did it work straightaway? No. It didn't. It was a disaster. It took six months to get it right but we bashed away at it. Tenacity.

"We just focused on the customer and what would make life better for them. Every time you open your fridge you've got delicious, healthy food in your fridge. Why? We know that people aren't getting any thinner, they're not getting any healthier, they loathe going to the supermarkets, supermarket produce isn't very fresh because it goes through a massive supply chain. Chemicals aren't very good for you and they're constantly being shown not to be very good for you. And we delicately develop the product around it.

And we do it very carefully and very well. It's got to be beautifully designed, it's got to be distinctive, it's got to be innovative, it's got to be within our ethical boundaries, etc.

"For example, we introduced a programme so that every delivery for the first 12 weeks they get something really special, that was a surprise. That transformed three-month retention. Absolutely transformed it. It had been declining for four years before we came back in and it suddenly just went up to where it was four years ago. It's all about simple, little things."

This is additional product innovation to go out to the same channel?

"But not massively, you know, not ground changing. Everything was about the detail and Abel & Cole will continue growing doing what it's doing. It's growing about 15% at the moment which, given the size of the business, is a very, very healthy period of growth.

"We are improving all the time on little things, little innovations that were really good fun, like we started making soup out of our leftovers. We started making our own juices. Our own brand stuff that sort of complemented what we were doing. We've got our Abel & Cole juices, our Abel & Cole soups. Our meat's now labelled Abel & Cole. Our milk's joint labelled so it's Barclay Farm and Abel & Cole. So it just all feels unique and individual."

In conversation with Rupert Lee-Browne

Rupert, so you have a successful business sending currency abroad based on robust system and process. Tell me about the innovation of that initial product.

"We've always tried to be ahead of the pack. One example is this: five years ago or so we looked into our clients' activity and discovered that they tended to trade with us every two and a half years. We wanted to introduce a product that enabled us to talk to them in the intervening time, would keep us front-of-mind but was still fundamentally based on our core competence of foreign exchange. We looked at a variety of things, none of which were very satisfactory.

"But we happened to land on pre-paid cards which, at the time, were expensive and very inefficient for the customer. It was a market dominated by two major institutions but we believed that there was an opportunity for us to create a great product for our own clients. So we created a good value pre-paid currency card for using when travelling overseas.

"It's simple. You load money on to it and we exchange the money into, for example, euro. When you travel, you use that card just like a bank debit card for buying things or to withdraw cash at ATMs. The benefit is that you have fixed the exchange rate when you loaded the card and you are not caught out with any extra charges. When you have used up the funds on it you can then reload it. We reckoned we could undercut the competitors on price but also make money at it – just by taking slimmer margins. Fantastic idea.

"So we launched this specifically for our customers with no real intention of it being particularly big. However, a few of our customers are journalists who liked what we were doing and very kindly wrote about it in their respective papers. Suddenly we started getting applications from people who weren't clients. And so the whole division mushroomed."

This product – the pre-paid card – serves a different market need. I'm not going to be buying my house on a pre-paid card.

"You're not. But if you have a house abroad or are looking to buy one then you necessarily are travelling overseas. Therefore you will need foreign currency for spending money."

So it's a perfect cross sell?

"It's a perfect cross sell. And that's what we've really concentrated on doing to make sure that we capture as great a share of the market as possible. From wealthy retirees who are moving overseas to business owners who are involved in international trade, all the way through to their teenage children travelling on their gap year. We're building a lovely niche in the upmarket, wealthy individuals at business owner/director level."

And what is the intellectual property that sits behind that innovation?

"It's the relationship with the customer."

What's product three then?

"Well, let's concentrate on getting products two and one right first."

In conversation with Roger Philby

Roger, I sense that you have a strong sense of your core assets. Can you tell me how that's enabled you to innovate in the business?

"So we started looking at our assets using the Seven Layers valuation framework. One of the challenges we have as a people consultancy is our valuation's kind of capped because our IP walks out the door every day and you hope it comes back in the morning. So, it's very hard to create equity value within a people consultancy. Traditionally the way you build your valuation is to drive up your revenues and your EBIT and you'll get a five to six times multiple and that all feels nice. But that wasn't enough for us. We wanted to also drive our multiple."

On the basis that your valuation is a simple formula of P x M so driving both makes sense?

"Right. We started to look at one of the challenges we have with our products which is that they are quite *high touch*, which means that although we generate lots of value it can be perceived as quite expensive. And then we looked at our intent which is to 'create opportunities for everyone to be brilliant at work.' The way we were delivering our service meant that our clients were only paying for their senior managers to go through Chemistry's process on the Development and the Insight sides.

"So we could do with annuity revenue because it drives up the value of our business and we have an intent to create an opportunity for everyone to be brilliant at work but, if we're truthful with ourselves, we're creating a sub-set of people to be brilliant. So we needed to innovate how we went to market – our system of delivery.

"We needed to embed our IP in a piece of technology so that someone at their desk can assess themselves against the five box model and produce a report into how they could develop. And instead of charging per person for that, which is what all our competition do in the psychometric test base, why don't we charge a fixed licence fee? So they don't have a variable cost, it's fixed but it's annual and it's a three-year contract. Good for the client and for us it's annuity revenue. So we've just increased the multiple applied to our business because we have innovated our delivery system and we have firm contracts over a number of years.

"And then we use that system to innovate product. We created a new product called Crucible. So, if you're at O2 and you want a retail job you play a game online created by us, and as you're playing the game it's measuring you against the five box model for O2."

And that innovation is all done in-house?

"Yes, absolutely. We have creative people loving it and dedicated to our success and the success of our customers. I see that culture as driving the innovation.

"And now major clients are jumping on the platform. For example, one used to pay us to profile 80 of their senior managers and they loved it. But before we had the Crucible platform the other 650 salespeople we could not have helped. So now with Crucible we have created a product innovation that not only have we got the fees from the senior leaders but we're now generating an annuity fee per head across 650 people plus an annual licence fee all of which adds up to more than our initial *high touch product*. Our P2 is much more profitable than our P1, as you would say.

"So product innovation drives our valuation because it creates annuity income but it also ties in with our intent. At this one client we can now help 740 people be brilliant at work instead of just 80."

Based on your asset.

"Based on our asset."

Action plan: 10 things in 100 days

1. If your organisation is not naturally innovative then once your commercial and cultural platform is in place, it's important to invest some real focus in this at the top of your organisation. **A 100 days of innovation project** driven by you but involving everyone might be a good way to kick off.

2. **Make a bold declaration of intent**. Think big. Make it fun.

3. Involve your customers and suppliers. **Ensure innovation is focused widely**. Gather and use lots of data.

4. Divide the task up functionally and **have people volunteer to join innovation teams**. Make sure these are well led and encourage those who agree to lead. Give plenty of autonomy but show your passionate involvement. Acknowledge people for their commitment and for their ideas. Remember innovations can be iterative and radical, cultural and commercial.

5. Whatever else you seek to innovate, it's critical to **make your business system a key focus and ask if it is the best it can be**. Be as creative as you can be, get out of the existing pattern, use analysis and ask customers and suppliers.

6. **Ask yourself if any of your current systems are, or could be, an asset** in their own right. Get creative. Sure, you designed them in a P&L context, but could they be or become an asset? How could you derive revenue or other value from them?

7. **Innovate your product iteratively**. Generate lots of ideas to ensure the customers' experience of the product is the best it can be. Never rest.

8. **Innovate your product radically**. Get really creative based on a fundamental understanding of your IP (assets). If that requires you to get really clear about the assets and drivers of your business that is a good topic for a retreat. Based on those assets what might people give you money for? What completely new product innovations could you create? Are there products hidden in your systems?

9. **Ensure your innovations programme includes your customer service strategy**. As part of the platform you devoted some focus to servicing customers between sales. How can you now

innovate that service to constantly improve and impress? What creative and fun ideas can you generate?

10. **Get management out of the pattern**. Don't be a Wenham Lake Ice Company. Find ways of stretching your perspective: educate yourself, read widely, meet interesting people, make the time.

Chapter 8.
The Gorilla in the Beehive

"Any business is chock full of innovative extension ideas. Owners just get stuck in the product they have to sell today."

Frank Bastow

Unlocking the power of extension

V+7	Scale
V+6	Brand architecture
V+5	Channel extension
(V+4)	Product extension
V+3	Systems / product innovation
V+2	Talent / capability / culture
V1	—————————— Industry benchmark

THE PREVIOUS CHAPTER WAS CONCERNED WITH INNOVATION OF systems and product, both in terms of iterative changes and creative leaps, exploring the impact on both the P&L and the asset value.

In this chapter I want to continue the innovation theme and introduce the next *layer of value* – product *extension*. This layer could have an exponential impact on the valuation of your business, but it is also by far the hardest to implement of all the layers we have explored so far. Consequently it is a layer relatively few companies successfully fully implement.

It has been very interesting talking to the Alchemists and seeing how far each has taken their businesses through the Seven Layers. All have built a superb platform that is independent of the leadership team and productive in both people and process terms. If they had not they would not be Alchemists. All have built a highly effective culture and focused resources and creativity on their talent and capability. All have innovated their product iteratively, or occasionally radically, and have innovated their system. Yet, despite all having superb businesses, each worth north of £10m and some many times that, the stories about genuine *extension* are fewer.

This tells me that it is a hard thing to do for most businesses and you can build a great business on product one and innovations of that. It's also true that all these businesses are on a journey up the Seven Layers and have plenty of headroom left.

I mentioned before that, at this point in the economic cycle, innovation is key; those companies that innovate win. However, the most dramatic gains are for those companies that effectively *extend* their product into the recovery phase. These are the ones that will grab share, create growth and build wealth faster than those that focus on the status quo.

Extension is key to maximising asset value at any point in the cycle. It's just that right now, and for the next couple of years, the opportunity to create completely new products and enter new markets and channels is wide open as competitors are still inwardly focused and customers are looking for new solutions.

Whether it's the iPod in 2001, Gillette Sensor in the early 1990s, Commerce Bank in 1973, or IBM in the long depression of 1873, every serious depression stimulates a crop of radical new products and emergent companies.

From the potato to the veg box

In innovation terms the path of least resistance is to extend your product logically. As an example, Apple extended *logically* from the revolutionary ("1000 songs in your pocket") iPod in 2001, through Mini (2004), Shuffle and Nano (2005), and Touch (2007). Essentially these are innovations of the same core product offering. For Keith Abel, it was a *logical* extension from the potato to organic potatoes to other vegetables in season to vegetable boxes.

There is absolutely nothing wrong with logical extension. For most businesses it is absolutely the right thing to do. It is right to focus on the product you know and to build a powerful business with an exceptional and to-purpose system and focused culture with the talent to deliver it. It is right to build a strong channel relationship and, most critically, for fabulous and loyal customers to buy it. This is the story of Abel & Cole and Caxton FX, amongst many others.

Nick Jenkins at Moonpig.com articulates this perfectly:

> "Obviously we looked at what else we could sell to our customers. But the track record of businesses trying to upsell and cross-sell is pretty poor. And you risk diluting your own business and annoying your customers. People knew what the Moonpig.com brand was about.

> "We started off by making sure that the Moonpig.com brand was absolutely focused on being a place you could get a really, really cool greetings card. And then we added flowers because flowers were just a natural complement. Buy a really, really cool greeting card and get some flowers to go with it. And gradually we built appropriate gifts into the mix so that now maybe a third of our revenue comes from gifts."

Extensions based on core assets

So much for logical extensions, but there comes a point at which the *assets* in the business can be leveraged to take a creative leap into whole new opportunities. This leap creates enormous value for the business. This is the gorilla in the beehive.

It's a gorilla because there are ideas in your business of huge power but you are all too busy rushing around the beehive to see them. The gorilla just sits there waiting to be noticed. To really see it, you need the right formula. And that formula sits in the assets we have been looking at throughout this book.

If this is true, why don't more companies achieve effective extension? Partly this is about mindset, the pattern is for *logical* extension. After all, our experience to date has reinforced that the current product works, so why risk change? The pattern is to rush around the beehive doing what we have done successfully for years. Partly it is received wisdom – *stick to the knitting*, we are told. Our innate conservatism is reinforced when we see so many examples of businesses that try new things and fail. It's safer not to notice the gorilla.

Sometimes there is a significant investment to be made to achieve an extension. This investment can be hard to achieve and carries a risk. I think this is why so many successful entrepreneurial companies sell to large corporates at this level. They know they need the resources of a much larger player to really drive the extension strategy.

So, there are reasons *not* to extend. Yet, we know the scale of the opportunity if we do and we get it right. So what is the answer? What is the source of an extension that is a creative leap whilst also being really successful? Where do you start?

The answer lies in understanding and strategically managing your key assets and planning your extension strategy from these assets. Put another way, from your true *intellectual property* (IP). Extensions based on your intellectual property create exponential value growth; extensions based on *product logic* create iterative value growth.

Incidentally, extensions based on a whim usually create no growth at all. Unless you just get lucky, if you jump into a hole in the market without your asset strategy in support, it could be a long fall. I think the fear of that fall puts a great many businesses off making the creative leap in the first place.

Understand your IP

To remove the fear, base your strategy on your IP. By this, I don't mean things you can register at the Intellectual Property Office. I mean the unique combination of knowledge, talent, experience, relationships, culture, reputation, technology, systems and belief that sits in your business. I mean the rocket juice in your business. Marshalling that IP to drive your extension strategy comes as near to guaranteeing success as it's possible to get.

You may not have heard of the brilliant scientist Ilya Prigogine. His research into the energy associated with chemical reactions and his studies of *complexity* won him the Nobel Prize in 1997. To me what is most interesting about him, since I have limited interest in chemical reactions, is that he also wrote a book about traffic management and became a leading light in the science of people flow.

The point is that he realised that his unique IP in understanding how order can be created from disorganised energy flows could be transferred to a completely unrelated field. In other words he creatively extended by focussing on IP and not on the existing *product* field.

The key to this trick is to understand the *context* of your IP: how can you define or encapsulate your IP in one word, or a few words? What is the defining rocket fuel that drives your business? I mentioned Jim Collins' *Good to Great* in an earlier chapter and his thesis that three key principles drive business greatness:

1. Understand what you can be best in the world at.

2. Understand your key economic drivers.

3. Understand what you believe in and are deeply passionate about.

What you are best in the world at is, to me, your IP (the other two we covered earlier in the book).

Identifying your true IP is, for most of us, exceptionally hard. Putting your finger on what you are best in the world at and defining this in a few short words is a tough call when you are inside the business. But that knowledge can be genuinely transformational if you can achieve it.

You can use some of the ideas discussed in the previous chapter to get creative around this. My own experience is that you need external help because it's often a lot more obvious to an outside observer.

Don't get stuck in the product you have to sell today

It is very easy to conflate your product with the IP that sits behind it. For instance, at Shirlaws we knew very well *what* we did. We are an international SME business coaching company. This did not help us to understand the true IP. I may be dim but I kept tripping up on the product. In the end I engaged outside advice to help us understand our true value proposition. Getting a handle on this was our doorway to understanding our true IP.

And the result?

Our IP is that we *understand the entrepreneur* and can therefore help them build powerful businesses and fulfilled lives, which is what we call "more money, more time, less stress". Our assets are all contained within and contribute to that IP; our innovative business tools and methodologies (product), systems of delivery, a unique culture and talent pool of ex-CEOs that deliver our stuff to clients, etc.

This insight may not seem all that radical from the outside. But the articulation of it felt fairly radical to me at the time. I hope that makes the point – I rarely meet a business that can articulate their true IP, yet it can sometimes be relatively easy to see from the outside.

From an asset extension perspective, how did this insight help me in running the business? Actually it was quite revolutionary. Imagine running the business against IP of *SME business coaching*. Our product and our market would therefore be obvious and this would involve successfully building a business servicing small business owners around the world. Innovatory product and systems could be put in place to deliver to this market.

Imagine, on the other hand, running the business against IP of *understanding the entrepreneur*. A whole set of new opportunities spring up; extension opportunities. These extensions are in addition to our core business. *Understanding the entrepreneur* still drives our existing product and market – we continue to focus passionately on the SME market – but we can now have a conversation with a host of other prospective customers.

These customers are not interested in SME business coaching (our product P1) but they are very interested in our assets of understanding the entrepreneur. They are very interested in learning the skills to engage more effectively with business owners, so we now have a training proposition for commercial banks, for example. They are very interested in how to think more like an entrepreneur, so we now have a culture change product for large organisations seeking to have the kind of agility and innovative ability that is characteristic of entrepreneurs.

As any extension product should be, these new products are remarkably scalable. They are built on exactly the same IP as the initial product. Yet they do not detract from or replace that product but, rather, enhance it.

What are you the best in the world at?

Let me give you another example.

A few years ago now, I was asked by a large accountancy firm to advise a client of theirs. This was a private business engaged in the removal of asbestos. The market was under extreme margin pressure and was in decline. The owners were worn down, they were facing the Second Brick Wall, and they wanted an exit. Their accountants had given them a very gloomy valuation.

Having got this far in this book, it will be apparent why that was: the business was under revenue pressure, the management team were tired (and the business reliant upon them) and the external factors were running against the business as they were in a declining market. In other words, the business failed in layers *below the line* which prevented it, in valuation terms, from even reaching benchmark.

Whatever strengths they had above the line (their assets) were relatively irrelevant. It was actually a really sad story as in many ways it was a great business and the owners had done a lot right. They had just not innovated in time and then had become disillusioned.

So, what was the solution? The question to ask is "What are you best in the world at?" although, given their state of disillusionment, I think I asked "What are you really good at?" The response was, inevitably, "asbestos removal". It is so hard to see beyond the product, particularly if a business has been built around that product year-on-year.

However, after a lot of conversation, a set of assets began to emerge; they had a fabulous culture of committed people, they were brilliant at training their own people and had invested in facilities to do that, they were great at recruiting and developing skilled labour, they understood complex UK and European legislation, they had great relationships with local authorities, they understood how to remove and dispose of toxic waste, and had a transport fleet fit for that purpose, etc. Already a list of assets is emerging – *a set of IP*.

When I asked them to look at that list and tell me what they saw and what they might imagine a company with that IP would *do* (product), they came up with quite a list from recruitment to training to consulting. These are their potential extensions and, since they are based on their IP, they are fairly likely to succeed. In the end they built a new business disposing of low-grade waste from council tips.

All great extension occurs where companies have truly understood their IP and have harnessed that to launch ambitious new extension products.

I love the Saga story. Saga is a UK travel company that started with a hotel and built a successful travel brand through bus and eventually packaged air travel. The marketplace they developed, whether by accident or design, was the over 50s age group. And here is the choice. If you look at this company from a product perspective, the logic is to innovate travel products. In that case you would probably wish to innovate out of the over-50s market. However, if you look more creatively at the company and from an asset perspective you realise that the core IP is actually based on an understanding of and relationship with that over-50s demographic.

From that perspective, your extension strategy looks very different. This is, I think, quite a leap when you are inside a travel company, but Saga, to their credit, reached that depth of insight into their business, which allowed them to extend their product into insurance and then other financial services, magazines and thereafter other media, etc., and build a multi-billion valuation business based on services for the over-50s. Had they *logically* extended into additional travel products (18 to 30s holidays?) I wonder where the business would be now.

What of Apple? If the iPod story is one of logical product innovation, where is the extension? The answer is obviously the iPhone, sales of which swiftly outstripped the iPod, then the iPad, Apple TV, etc. These are genuinely different products. These are *extensions*.

To extend logically or creatively?

If you look at these two big contextual themes – to innovate the product logically, or to extend creatively based on your IP – the question to ask is whether you would increase equity more quickly through a logical next step extension or by understanding your fundamental assets and extending from those. Both are perfectly sound strategies. Which serves you best in equity terms at this point in your business?

Let's look at real-life example of a medical supplies company with £12.8m of revenue and £2m of profit. The management team wanted to reach £24m of revenue to double its profit. To achieve this they could, contextually, explore two alternatives:

1. Instead of a medical supplies company, they could think of themselves as *a supplies company with one business in the medical space*. Against that, what other business lines could they develop which relate to being really *good at supplies*?

2. Or they could imagine running a *medical company*. All their assets – knowledge and contacts – now relate to the medical industry, rather than being good at supplies. If they are now a medical company, with one business in medical supplies, what else might they do?

In this case, the company chose to go for the second option and focusing on the business assets stimulated loads of new ideas for extension. Once the management team recognised themselves as a medical business rather than a supplies business, they really began to create masses of innovative possibilities – medical recruitment, for example. When asked whether it would be faster to build a supplies business from £12m to £24m or a medical business, their answer was immediate. Asset extension of a medical business would be faster.

What this suggests to me is the value of asking yourself the "What if?" question in relation to how you define your business. "What if we were a xx business? Then what would we do?" is a great question because the next question can be "How would we extend from there?"

I have been looking at the property market recently with the aim of building a portfolio to let. I have been struck by how almost all the companies I have talked to started as property sales businesses (estate agents or realtors) and then extended into letting alongside the main business. Most didn't seem particularly good at lettings. I think what is happening is that a successful property broker looks for the next business and jumps into a logical hole called lettings but without considering his or her assets. It's a logical extension but certainly not an asset extension.

If we look at property brokering businesses, they are actually sales businesses. Lettings businesses, on the other hand, are administration businesses. The staff in property businesses are sales and marketing people, whose chief skill-set is not administration. This means that property businesses unwittingly set sales people, with very poor administration skills, to run an administration business. They make less money than they expect because sales and administration skills are diametrically opposed. I have found one specialist lettings business which doesn't do property sales and they are brilliant.

For property brokers, therefore, the "What are you best in the world at?" question is likely to have a response around sales skills and local knowledge/connections. The next question to find the extension *might* therefore be more along the lines of "What else can we sell locally?" rather than "What else can we do in property?"

For other businesses the question might be "Who do you know?" or "What do you know?" Our asbestos company, for example, knew the local authorities really well and had a lot of skills appropriate to their broad waste needs.

So far, we have looked at extension very much in commercial terms. But, as the asbestos story shows, there can be a huge impact culturally on you and your team as well.

The extension journey normally occurs after the business has emerged from the Second Brick Wall; the business has its core product, position and functional systems in place with a capable team and good cultural platform. Owners and management teams become intensely energised by new possibilities. Most business owners describe their feeling at this point as intensely and fundamentally *proud*.

As the medical supplies business said: "We never saw our business in this way before. We feel completely re-energised about this new asset approach."

The Alchemist's view

In conversation with Russell Stinson

Russell, tell me more about when you began to think about extending your business.

"We were looking at luxury home cleaning and a franchising model. We knew we were capable of doing things and doing them very, very well, but our exploration of this extension wasn't a very joined-up strategy. It was more 'This is our core capability, this is what we're capable of doing, let's try this.' It was a little bit opportunistic."

I think that's very typical. You see there's an opportunity and you jump right in. But it's not based on your core asset. It just looks like a good punt.

"Yes. That's exactly it. When we did our retreat and looked at the big strategic picture we asked ourselves searching questions such as – 'Is this the right thing for you? Does this fit with your intent to make a difference? With your values? With what you're trying to do? It was crystal clear that it simply didn't fit with the value proposition, with our IP; the alignment was so far away. We came back and made the decision on the Monday to stop it. So it was that crystal clear that it was not aligned with where we're looking to go as a business and our future."

In conversation with Frank Bastow

Frank, you've described how you took a traditional family building and decorating firm and built a commercial and cultural platform. You created a culture with a clear intent and that makes your management team independent of you and a culture of innovation that systemises the business to make it easy. So now you describe yourself as having all the time in the world and are now on a mission to build assets. Tell me about that.

"What we're really good at is creating red systems and productising them. We are really good at simplifying the back office. When I took a really hard look at the true assets in the business – our intellectual property – actually it had nothing to do with painting or renovating buildings. We are good at that, but that's just one product.

"What sits behind that is a genius at simplifying back-office processes. And when I had a bit of head space – when we got the business into *advanced growth* – I realised we could create products based on that IP. We've done it twice; we've done it with accountancy and with HR. Our ability, our IP, is to create new red products that work so well they give the customer complete peace of mind because that's what we have always done in our own business. Because I hate hassle."

That's quite a creative leap from building services to business systems and HR systems.

"Yeah, but I believe any business is chock-full of innovative extension ideas. It's just that the owners get stuck in the product they happen to sell today. So they never create all the wealth and make things better in the world. They get stuck. It's daft, isn't it?"

This is about assets?

"It is, yeah. That's the only thing that's important to me: assets. I have an irrelevancy with income, that's why in any new business I'm not interested in getting in income, all I'm looking for is building assets. I want to make people money while they sleep. Assets do that. It's all I'm ever interested in. Also, it's more fun."

Tell me about your extensions.

"Azure started about a year ago. When we liberated our old financial director, she went off to do her own thing; I thought 'This is a red function. I know it's terrifying, but, if it's red, I should be able to outsource it and then manage the relationship.' So I looked for a great cost-management accountant and then we built a system with him. It was fantastic in terms of costs saved and productivity. I looked at it and I went, 'Hang on, if it's good for us, we should be able to do this for anybody else,' so that's when I went into business with him. So we did a deal, built up the client base.

"We've got six girls who work on the basis that they're qualified accountants, as well as being mothers who work part time, so we need a great online system to track and run all that. We've got about 110 clients so far and that's growing fast – we could double our turnover this year. We give customers absolute peace of mind, which is a brand promise in all my businesses. You want to be able to say 'We need that sorted out.' You don't have to make a file note, it just gets done."

Is that part of your core IP?

"Yes, it comes of looking after high-end people in smart parts of London. It's part of the IP of creating absolute peace of mind and putting the system behind that. Because if you have somebody down at Eaton Square, they don't ring Grosvenor Estates up, they ring the Duke of Westminster up. They're mates. Imagine the pressure of looking after clients on that estate. So we made sure we never let anyone down. Not ever.

"Hindsight came out eight months ago. I met this brilliant guy with amazing ideas in software development. You don't need all the detail but it's solution-testing software. When you write software you always get to the end and know you could have done it twice as fast and twice as well with hindsight. We provide that hindsight at the start of the process! So we called the company Hindsight. Last month we sold five deals to absolutely top multinational companies.

"And the other one is Treacle Tiger which also came out of an asset that we created in Bastows. We realised we were great at developing cultures, training and HR, so we turned that into a product. When we got the Health and Wellbeing Award (we were the second firm within the M25 to get that – Claridge's got it first), we thought, 'Hang on, we've spent all this time and effort and money on this, isn't that something we could sell out as a product?'"

You have a decorating and maintenance business, an accountancy outsourcing business, a software business and an HR business. Some of those businesses service the biggest corporations in the world and others work in UK SME. Frank, MBAs will be foaming at the mouth screaming "What's the core competence?"

"No, it all makes perfect sense. It's the IP. It's what I've learnt along the way about systems and simplification. It's all bundled together in that concept of simplifying red through systemising it. It doesn't matter what or who. It matters to me that we serve our intent to nurture – to make stuff better. It matters that we make it easier by creating a system. And I've got a multi-million pound group of companies and have given opportunities to hundreds of people and still have all the time in the world so, to be honest, I don't give a stuff what they think."

Action plan: Things to do in the next 100 days

1. It's a good time to revisit the layers below where your business is now. To extract real value from a layer you **must have fully implemented strategies in the all the layers underneath**.

2. To continue the asset journey, ask yourself the question of whether you would increase equity more quickly through a logical next step extension or by understanding your fundamental assets and extending from those. A good question to ask is "What if we were a xyz company? Then what would we do?"

3. The extension strategies that create the most exponential value growth are sourced in an understanding of the core IP. A great topic for a quarterly retreat is to get a real understanding of your IP and be able to articulate it in a few words. Part of this is **understanding what you can be best in the world at**.

4. Use that understanding of your IP to **drive and strategically manage your product extension strategy**. List all of your core asset drivers, all the elements of your IP, and ask yourself what a company with those assets would do. What products would it make and sell? Use that insight to drive an extension strategy conversation.

5. Make sure you can **see beyond your product**. Use all the innovation techniques to get the perspective you need to really see what sits behind your current product and proposition.

6. **Think about what and who you know** more than what you do.

7. You may be well served by **getting some external perspective**. It's often incredibly hard to identify the true IP in your business and not get tied up in your product. It's often easier to see it from the outside.

Chapter 9.
New Fronts

"Entrepreneurs shouldn't be afraid of partnerships and collaborations of all types."

Ajaz Ahmed

"Now we're getting ambitious. Now we're thinking we could disrupt the entire psychometric test market which is worth nine billion pounds annually."

Roger Philby

Innovating your channel assets

V+7	Scale
V+6	Brand architecture
(V+5)	Channel extension
V+4	Product extension
V+3	Systems / product innovation
V+2	Talent / capability / culture
VI	————————————— Industry benchmark

THE PREVIOUS CHAPTER CONCLUDED WITH A GREAT COMMENT from Frank Bastow which summarises where we have got to so far:

"It matters to me that we serve our intent to nurture – to make stuff better. It matters that we make it easier by creating a system. And I've got a multi-million pound group of companies and have given opportunities to hundreds of people and still have all the time in the world so, to be honest, I don't give a stuff what they think."

Frank and his team have built a successful and profitable business. But, far more importantly, it's a valuable (high multiple) business because they have focussed on their core assets building, as Frank explains, a powerful culture (V+2) based on their intent, a world-class system (V+3) which they have then leveraged into innovative product extensions, sometimes in the form of standalone businesses (V+4). Frank Bastow is the absolute exemplar of the entrepreneur who has built his pyramid of assets with such strong cultural and system foundation layers that he has "all the time in the world" to create more and more opportunities for himself and his commercial family.

Once again, this is a choice. How far you choose to progress through these layers is up to you. For some businesses staying at V+2 or V+3 is all they need to do in order to achieve the creatively fulfilling, valuable business they want whilst preserving the life-balance they need.

Remember that each of these layers takes *time* – usually years not months – and, the further up you climb, increasingly can require *investment*.

It is also imperative to reiterate that, in order to extract real value from a layer you *must have fully implemented* the layers below. Of course you can innovate products without adequate talent or a great self-responsible culture, but these innovations are less likely to be truly sustainable and won't generate full value. You can extend your product into wildly creative areas without developing the pattern of innovation in your business products and systems but the extension is likely not to be based on a true understanding of your assets and is thus less likely to succeed and be truly sustainable.

My experience of running my business through the seven layers process was that we spent a lot of time back-filling and polishing areas we had tried in the past and got half-right. It was a really engaging process as it all felt consistent and as if every element of the business was running in the same strategic direction.

And it took time. In fact, for our business, it took nearly three years to get to V+4 and we are likely to spend another couple of years making *channel* – which is V+5, the area to which we now turn our attention – really work for us.

What do I mean by channel and what does making a channel work involve?

There is no mystery to this. The channel is the *path through which goods and services travel from vendor to consumer.* The strategic bit is just thinking creatively and innovatively about which channels are appropriate and available for each of your products and businesses. If you innovate and extend a product, the next question is what *channels* can you create or innovate for it?

The reason this is an asset conversation, of course, is that the long-term return on developing expertise, relationships and security into a new channel is likely to be exponential. If valuation is essentially based on a view of future discounted cash, the more channels you develop the greater the asset value.

There is another aspect to this as well. Very often the development of channels can be complex, time-consuming and expensive. It can be a real distraction to the business and is not entered into lightly. You may recall that after Keith Abel sold his business, the new owners devoted time and treasure to trying to develop a new channel in retail. This was not based on the IP and assets of Abel & Cole and was doomed to failure. It is only now, years later, that a much larger Abel & Cole is beginning to seriously explore a new asset-based channel for the brand and it isn't in retail.

A number of the Alchemists commented on how complex and expensive creating the channel called *going international* has been. Even Moonpig.com has only expanded into two other major markets because Nick didn't believe his IP supported further extension. The experience of Shirlaws, too, has been that expanding to having offices in 11 countries has been slow and relatively cautious. It took 12 years for us to open our first office in a non-English speaking country.

If you think about some of the sales of entrepreneurial businesses to large corporates, the element the business was missing (and the outcome the sale achieved) was the development of significant new *channels*.

Caution is therefore the watchword. But the ability to develop channels can represent a truly significant asset over and above the outcome of the channel itself. In other words, your business becomes a lot more valuable to a potential partner or acquirer because of a proven ability to develop channels. Put simply, your expertise, relationships, etc., can hugely enhance the return from the product of this partner or acquirer.

Whether you see your new channel strategy as an asset for your own business or as a means of attracting a future partner, it is a highly worthwhile strategic initiative. So long as your supporting assets are fully in place.

Of course, some channels are more complex than others. Some products are easier than others. As with product extension, your channel extension must be based on your IP. You will struggle to jump into a new channel without that leap being supported by your core assets.

What a channel looks like

So, what could a channel look like?

It could be anything that efficiently gets your goods to your target customer. Most of this will be terribly obvious but, for the sake of completeness, here is a short and far from comprehensive list:

- Direct selling

- Indirect selling (including advertising, exhibitions, etc.)

- Fixed retail

- Online and mobile retail

- Wholesale

- Agencies

- Informal partnerships – distribution

- Formal partnerships

- Licences

- Markets (sector, international, etc.)

The question is, of course, which of these can be best accessed given your current assets? Given your IP?

As this is an innovation it's important to do some analysis, as was discussed in Chapter 7. I used to run an outsourcing business which was reasonably successful but we felt we could be doing a lot more. Looking back I can see it as a classic *stuck at the Wall, below-benchmark, P&L-based, private business*, but at the time it just felt a bit like swimming through treacle, although it was paying the bills.

In an effort to get ourselves out of this situation, we began to think about who was selling our product when we weren't. This was designed to uncover our channel strategy and it revealed that we simply didn't have one. We were really a one-channel business. I remember the analysis we did which was to draw a spider diagram of all the channels we might develop and a simple cost/benefit analysis of each. We then looked at the assets and resources we had related to each channel. It took an afternoon and changed the business forever.

However you do your analysis it is important to get some data and KPIs to help you prioritise and measure your channel strategy.

This is absolutely not a book about the 'content' of channel management or sales strategies. If it was, I would not be writing it. But I do want to comment on the last four points of the above list of what a channel might look like from my own experience.

The sales force that does not ask to be paid

Firstly, let's take a look at *distribution* in the context of *informal relationships*. In my outsourcing business, when we did our analysis of our potential strategies, this is the channel that we found would give us the biggest return for the smallest investment. I think it's always worth considering before you move on to more complex channels. Essentially it's just a matter of thinking who could be proactively promoting your product on your behalf without being paid to do so. Who can be your unpaid salesforce?

We often think other companies will promote us if they have an immediate commercial return in doing so. That kind of channel is fine – it can be an agency arrangement or a formal commercial partnership – but don't discount the fact that there are people who will actively introduce you without payment and they are worth nurturing. It can be beneficial to develop this area strategically.

Who are these white knights and how do you find them? It's not hard. They are people who are already in a trusted relationship with your target customer. If they could be persuaded to introduce your product, this third-party introduction from a trusted source will have huge influence.

If not for immediate financial reward, why would someone refer or recommend you? The most obvious answer is because they believe in what you do, which is why it is fairly key to really understand yourself what it is that you believe in. They might be customers who have experienced your product. They might equally be people who supply other services to your customers. In both cases their reward is to help out the person they refer you to.

As Nick at Moonpig.com discovered, there is sometimes no need to reward customers for referrals; they will refer if they believe in your product. The same is true of other potential channel partners. All of Shirlaws' work comes from referral and a lot of that is from accountants, lawyers and bankers who have no expectation of reward but simply want their customers to do well. Equally we refer customers to other advisors we believe in.

Once you have identified who your target customers trust (this might be the *crowd* in a B to C world, but the principle is the same) is it just a matter of educating them about what you do? Not really. It's not about selling benefits; it's more about sharing *why* you do it, sharing your beliefs and passion and giving them an experience of what makes you the *best in the world* at what you do.

However, most fundamentally, it is about overcoming the reasons why they would not recommend you. As a customer these fears are already largely overcome. But as a distribution partner you need to work to overcome their natural fears. These fears can be listed and, if you like, openly discussed. Based on hundreds of relationships I can tell you that human fears boil down to five:

1. Trust

2. Control

3. Quality

4. Consistency

5. Time

If you can overcome all these fears and simultaneously engage a partner in what you really believe and care about you may have created an unpaid sales force. And every time you recommend a product you believe in you do the same for someone else.

I have a story about taking my two boys to rugby training on Sundays that explains these fears pretty well. The first time I took them, I got chatting to another dad on the touchline. Over subsequent Sundays we talked more and more, and eventually started going to each other's homes after training (for a snack for the kids and a beer for us).

After a while, this other dad offered to pick up the boys one Sunday to save me from going down to the ground and I said yes. So far so normal. But imagine if, on that first day, this stranger had offered to pick up my boys the following Sunday. Would I have accepted? The only difference here is that we had time to overcome fears and develop a relationship.

Exactly the same principle applies in professional relationships. Work out how you can give your potential distribution partners an experience of you, your values and your beliefs, and work through all the fears that could derail the relationship. It will pay dividends.

Marriage can be a sentence not a word

I mention informal partnerships because they are relatively low risk and very often overlooked. Although well worth investing some strategic attention to, in an asset space, informal distribution is useful but unlikely to be of massive significance. It is probably insufficiently scalable and hard to define.

Formal partnerships, on the other hand, offer rather obvious benefits. I mentioned in a previous chapter the wonderful Annabel Karmel, the baby food entrepreneur. Annabel's product and channel extension story is of the classic form as she innovated from selling baby food in retail, to selling recipe books online, to apps and so on.

What Annabel did exceptionally well, however, was to link up with a wide range of channel partners including the obvious retailers but also airlines and sports clubs. It's a story of looking at your assets creatively and seeing what you have that others want. It's scarcely worth saying that partnering with a larger trade partner or one with different assets can be a fast track to saleable, profitable revenues and enhanced valuation. This does not have to be a merger but can simply be a trading relationship. Of course, such a trade partnership could also be a partial sale (M&A).

Naturally, partnership has accompanying risks. According to *Harvard Business Review*, between 70% and 90% of mergers fail, which suggests that a very high proportion of commercial partnerships of all types fail.

The reasons are inevitably a mismatch in expectations and assets. A truly open conversation about expectations is key going in – and knowledge of the five fears I mentioned above can help here. Equally, each partner must understand its own assets and that of the other. Each must have a clear sense of its IP and how this will work in collaboration with the other's.

The canard is that partnerships fail because of *culture*. This is, of course, true, but as we have already established, culture is just an asset. Culture (and most particularly intent and values) must be complementary as must the other assets so that, at each level, the partnership is consistent, energising and fair.

A marriage doesn't fail because the couple are too different from each other. It fails because they are not complementary; they are not aligned.

Earning while you sleep

I have already covered in a number of places the idea that your assets are valuable partly because of their value to someone else – someone who will exchange the ownership or partial-ownership of those assets for significant cash through a partial or total sale of the business. Of course, there is another way to extract value from your assets without sacrificing ownership. That is through licensing.

It is well worth getting innovative in seeing if you can package your assets in such a way that someone else would pay handsomely to use them. That might be through leveraging your brand, which we will cover briefly in the next chapter, or through white labelling your engine, service or product.

The latter is the most obvious; can one or more of your existing products be packaged such that it can be licensed to someone else? Once again, the rules of innovation covered in Chapter 7 apply in terms of thinking creatively and broadly about this. Look at opportunities in other sectors and other jurisdictions. Look at successful licensing deals elsewhere and see what you might learn.

Less obviously perhaps, are there other assets in your business that you can package and license to others? You may recall that Frank Bastow created a new business out of his innovation in his back-office system. This kind of innovation could equally be a licensing opportunity.

The simple fact is that if you have IP in your business there is the chance at least that you can license it to someone else.

Going global

It is quite remarkable how many successful businesses, in mature markets at least, fail to internationalise. The truth is that, for many, it is one of the hardest innovations to make, particularly if it means setting up foreign operations, engaging with overseas partners and dealing with opaque legislation.

Surveys of domestic business in countries all over the world reveal the same two principle factors that prevent SMEs internationalising: a lack of knowledge (and the fear that creates), and a lack of contacts and trusted relationships.

Yet it is equally clear that businesses that internationalise outperform those that don't.

So to exploit this channel, what do you need? The answer is, of course, appropriate assets in place.

- Do you have the culture in place to allow the senior team to devote sufficient time to develop overseas opportunities? Will your culture support overseas travel and all that brings with it? Do you have the talent and capabilities to internationalise, whether that means language skills or relevant experience?

- Will your systems support an international expansion? Are they robust enough? Are they designed for cross-border trade, invoicing, shipping, etc. Is your product appropriate for other markets and, if so, which markets? What innovations are required for this new channel?

- Would a product extension suddenly open up new markets overseas? In your strategy for extension, was this in your thinking?

So long as your assets are in place and are aligned with the opportunity, like any other innovation, you have a good chance of success. Then you just need to overcome the fears of your lack of knowledge and develop local contacts.

One place to start is with government. In the UK, the arm of government called UKTI (UK Trade & Investment) can be exceptionally helpful when they understand your needs. Equally, other advisors with international experience can be helpful.

One initiative that has really impressed me is the move to International Managers by HSBC. The bank is genuinely investing behind its *world's leading international bank* positioning. Businesses that I know who have an International Manager find he or she can plug them into an effective network and provide an invaluable international perspective. I'm quite sure it is not a panacea, and equally other banks may already have or may develop in the future a similarly international perspective, but it is good to see a bank trying to address its customers' needs and is well worth a look.

The Alchemist's view

In conversation with Ajaz Ahmed

Ajaz, can I ask you how partnership shows up for you at AKQA?

"In pretty much everything we do. I think we have built our business to well over half a billion of value on the basis of collaboration, partnership and healthy relationships. Those three things. None of our products can be built by one person. We must collaborate with each other, with suppliers, with other businesses and with customers."

So collaboration is about creating the best. Is it also about access to market? Is it about channel?

"Yes. Happy customers become your greatest source of business, either with them or with people they know. Smart partnerships and sometimes acquisitions are crucial. Thinking that you can figure it all out for yourself is futile. We have also always sought to collaborate with others to create the growth we wanted. In 2001 we partnered with Accenture – and they took a stake in us early on – and they helped us to become global.

"It's the same with WPP. We have been talking to them for years and it's an absolutely natural partnership. Being part of WPP gives us so much flexibility and freedom. It allows us to grow faster than ever before. The results speak for themselves. Entrepreneurs shouldn't be afraid of partnerships and collaborations of all types.

"I love to help other entrepreneurs when they have good values and are encouraging meritocracy and excellence. It's part of my idea of a virtuous circle. The feedback I get is that my advice has been of use but I also get so much out of it – they give me so many ideas and show me so many things that I am learning all the time."

In conversation with Roger Philby

Roger, you have been incredibly articulate about your asset strategy based on a powerful culture but with a clear strategy around innovation and extension. Tell me about your channel strategy within that context.

"OK. Based on our core asset? Well, we developed and innovated our core IP into a piece of technology that we can take into different channels. The problem with our physical IP is that it's tough to protect outside a controlled channel so we needed the lawyers looking at it. Anyway, the single biggest piece of innovation around our core IP has been the product extension into technology. That is having a dramatic impact on customers and our own business because now it is online it can reach far more people and it's giving us annuity income.

"So you look at that and you go 'Oh, so they moved their product online', but the real benefit is equity and value. Adding to this equity story, we're now pulling all this data into our own analytical tools so the next time a client goes 'We'd like to...', we go 'We've got benchmark data from 18 FTSE 100 companies, what do you want? Sales leaders? Sales people? Boom, boom, boom.'

"So we're now turning it into a sales tool. So, that's been incredible. And we're spending three quarters of a million pounds on it this year. We've hired a Head of Online who's sensational. We've moved some of our own people who know our IP really well into the online platform and they're really doing the thinking round that. It's got to the point where actually we're taking on the big players in the psychometric test market. And so, we're now getting ambitious. We're now thinking we could disrupt the entire psychometric test market which is worth nine billion pounds annually."

Action plan: 10 things in 100 days

1. This might be a good opportunity for the leadership team to pause and reflect; an opportunity to re-articulate your collective and personal visions and to check in how far you want to go both culturally and commercially. Very specifically, **do you want a multi-channel business and if so, what does that look like?**

2. Think creatively and innovatively about **which channels are appropriate and available for each of your products and businesses**. If you have innovated and extended a product, the next question is what channels can you create or innovate for it?

3. Do the analysis. Not all channels are equal. **Work out which channel will give you the most return for a given commercial and energetic investment**. Prioritise accordingly.

4. Consider whether your channel is an asset for you because it allows you to extend into new or higher-margin markets for your products, or whether a channel could be an asset for someone else. That could be an acquirer or commercial partner. **Think of yourself as a channel for someone else and ask 'What if?' questions**.

5. **Revisit your IP and use that understanding to drive and strategically manage your channel extension strategy**. List all of your core asset drivers, all the elements of your IP, and ask yourself what a company with those assets would do. What channels would it sell into? Use that insight to drive a channel extension strategy conversation.

6. **Don't ignore unpaid referrals as a source of pre-qualified leads**. Identify who can act as your channel, share what you believe in and overcome fears.

7. **Get digital**. If you are a foreigner in a digital world, find a native to guide you. That can be an external adviser, or a new hire. At Shirlaws we have loved bringing in interns; we give them a step into employment and they act as our guides in the digital world. Get innovative about the opportunities for you online.

8. Look at your assets and IP creatively and see what you have that others want. **Think about what partnerships will open new markets for you**. Think broadly and creatively.

9. How can you package your assets in such a way that someone else will pay handsomely for them? **What within your layers of assets (culture, talent, systems, product) could be valuable to someone else**? How might you structure a licence deal?

10. Take time to **consider the implications of going international**. Do you have the culture, capabilities, systems and products in place to open up international markets? If not, what do you need to innovate? Have any recent systems or product innovations opened up new opportunities overseas? Do you have the knowledge and trusted contacts in your chosen market? If not seek advice.

Chapter 10.
Brand Architecture

"Great brands are about smart and artful storytelling."

Ajaz Ahmed

Brand as an asset

V+7	Scale
(V+6)	Brand architecture
V+5	Channel extension
V+4	Product extension
V+3	Systems / product innovation
V+2	Talent / capability / culture
V1	———————————— Industry benchmark

THE STATED PURPOSE OF THIS BOOK WAS TO SHOW HOW TO build through and well beyond the first £10m; how to build an advanced growth, asset-focused, wealth-generative business that is easy to run and a joy to own. For almost all businesses, V+6 is beyond what is required to reach this level. It is beyond what most private businesses choose to achieve.

That is not to say that *brand* is not important and is not something practically every business spends time and some cash developing. It is to say that very few SMEs create a brand that is, of itself, *an asset*.

Brand plays a critical part in supporting a business' position in the market and the communication of what it does. Good branding can help drive sales, improve margins and recruit talent. In P&L terms it is a valuable investment and deserves considerable attention. It is not, however, the remit of this book to cover brand or branding at a *content level*. There are myriad great books on the subject. Seth Godin is always, in my opinion, well worth reading and his books *Purple Cow*, *Permission Marketing*, *Ideavirus* and *All Marketers are Liars* are all excellent. Philip Kotler is also thought-provoking and I would recommend *Kotler on Marketing*. Finally the book I have already mentioned, Simon Sinek's *Start with Why* is pure gold.

The purpose of this book is to look at a pyramid of assets and brand architecture sits at very nearly the top of this.

Creating your brand architecture

It is, of course, true to say that brand works at every one of the valuation layers in support of the other assets in the business. It is an integral part of your IP. It is a reflection of, and support for, your culture. It may support product innovation and extension. It will almost certainly play a huge part in your channel strategy.

It is therefore worth thinking about brand in asset or IP terms. Since, as a V+5 business owner, you know the intellectual property that powers the business, you therefore also understand the *architecture* that supports the brand. It is critical to see your brand from this perspective – is everything you are doing and saying communicated from this core IP? In the same way that extension can miss if not supported by this IP, branding can *miss* if the IP is misunderstood or not aligned.

I mentioned earlier that at Shirlaws we spent a lot of time clarifying our central IP as "we understand the entrepreneur." As brand architecture that insight gives us tremendous clarity. It creates the *why* that makes sense of the *what*. It is not the same as Shirlaws' intent ("to change lives"), but is closely allied to it. There is an important nexus between brand/position and intent/purpose.

What supports communication is then the *content* of our brand. This is the library of products, services, methodology, benefits, client experiences, etc. It is what we *do*. Before we got real clarity on our IP and started using that as our focus, we used to focus on all that content. The result was that our communication was somewhat muddled. And so were we.

If you think about a lot of successful big brands they have some fairly clear architecture which drives why they do what they do and therefore makes sense of the *what*. I'm not a branding expert but Amazon is all about innovation, Persil all about care, HSBC all about international, Zappos all about service, etc.

This is not rocket science, but it's amazing how many brands – particularly SME brands – focus on the content of what they do and not the architecture that makes sense of it. When did you last see any communication from a firm of lawyers, for example, that did not talk about their product expertise in lawyering?

With clear architecture, the fun part can be the *messaging*, or what is sometimes called marketability. What message do you have that can cut through all that clutter? Given that we only know the two tallest mountains in the world and forget all the rest, how can you ensure you are one of those two? To be distinctive you need to be different, whether that is challenging, amusing, surprising or quirky.

In talking to Keith Abel it was clear that his whole organisation had a clear understanding of this and every element of their communication, from the way the phone was answered, to the copy in the leaflets and recipes, to how the drivers looked, dressed and behaved, was consistently friendly, fun, quirky and engaging. It's a good idea to constantly challenge yourself around this area; is your communication based on your architecture and not your product? Is your communication marketable? Is the *whole* business and *everything* you do completely aligned and consistent around this?

Licensing the brand

Brand as an element that drives the P&L and brand that is part of the asset mix is fairly clear. But what of brand as a standalone asset? You know you have one of these when people give you money for it. Then it is a V+6 asset.

The most obvious example is where a third party uses your brand to sell their product. We talked earlier about licensing your product or system. This conversation is about deriving sustained income from *licensing your brand*.

We see this increasingly in the corporate world where a confectionary brand might license its name to an ice-cream manufacturer or an entertainment brand might license its brand to a toy manufacturer. When my kids were small, we used to have an off-road buggy branded Landrover. It had certainly never seen the inside of the plant at Solihull!

A really strong brand asset will also attract partners who want to use that strength to help them to access or grow their market. In this way your brand has essentially become a channel that you own.

At its most developed, your brand supersedes everything else and effectively *becomes* your IP. An example of this in action is Virgin, which is extraordinarily successful at leveraging its brand by taking minority interests in businesses that are consistent with its values and intent.

These businesses run relatively autonomously, derive huge value from the Virgin brand, and Virgin shares in the income and asset growth.

If you have a powerful brand and believe it is an asset, it is therefore a matter of thinking *innovatively* about how you can leverage this asset.

The obvious point, though, is that whilst brand is a hugely valuable asset, which is why it sits at the top of the pyramid, it also almost always represents a colossal investment in terms of years of sustained and consistent development and mountains of cash. Whilst we all have a brand, in the owner-managed business it is rare for it to be a genuinely standalone asset. Attempting to leverage a brand that is not a true asset is a pretty thankless task.

Even in the world of large multinationals I am always amazed at how lacking in innovation so many businesses are in leveraging their rather obvious brand asset in terms of channel (e.g. licensing) or product extension. For example, the Alchemists all have strong and well-regarded brands that are integral to their successful asset strategies. Yet, I would argue (with trepidation) that only the Abel & Cole and Moonpig.com brands are truly leverageable assets in their own right.

Of course there are huge risks in allowing someone else to use your brand. *Quality* and *control* fears come right to the fore! Consequently, this is a relatively high-cost and high-risk game with plenty of legal and other external advisors. Brand owners rightly tread cautiously in this arena.

Winding up JCB

I had occasion to see this risk for real with JCB. It's a slightly embarrassing story but worth telling. I had bought a JCB drill in a major DIY retailer and within a month the product had failed. I took it back to the retailer but was told that without the receipt they could do nothing despite the fact the product was exclusively sold by them. I rang JCB and was put through to a call-handling service (who told me that they were not JCB but just acted for them).

By this point I was somewhat frustrated and wrote to their Chief Executive effectively casting doubt on their commitment to their brand and highlighting the risks of licensing their hugely valuable brand willy-nilly to poor quality power tools manufacturers. From my perspective, here was a classic example of a big brand making a quick buck without due consideration to its brand assets both in terms of product quality and customer service. I regarded it as a classic case of the wrong extension and a brand asset detached from its core IP. Oh boy, how wrong I was.

At that point the entire, magnificent machinery of JCB swung into action. The CEO of their Consumer Division phoned me the next day and explained, with exceptional courtesy and patience but with steely resolve, that they did actually know what they were doing with their brand, that the drill manufacturer to whom they had licensed the brand was world-beating and that the product had been subject to two years of testing to ensure it met with the values and quality (IP) of the JCB brand and that mine was the first complaint they had received.

He told me that in service terms, yes, they used an external agency that, like JCB, was a family-run business and one they had used for years and trusted absolutely. Extraordinarily, the CEO knew exactly who I had spoken to at this agency. He was also going to take the matter up with the retailer, who should have resolved the complaint without question. We then had an absurdly British conversation during which I apologised and tried to refuse his offer of a replacement. He won and my drill arrived by courier the next day. It has been faultless ever since.

The point of this story is not to make the obvious (P&L) point that a complaint well handled creates an advocate (seriously, I urge you buy JCB products). The point is to unpick the assets sitting behind the story. JCB absolutely understand the value in their brand asset. They had built that brand over 50 years and had now reached the point where they could leverage the asset to generate scalable new income (and asset growth).

They had done this from the perspective of their IP and with extreme caution. They had innovated product extensions (from earth movers to domestic tools) and innovated a new channel (an exclusive deal with the DIY retailer) and, again, these innovations had been based on their core IP. That is why they reacted so strongly when I, naively, suggested the extension strategy was undermining the brand.

I also had an insight to the strength of the systems JCB must run. It was easy for the CEO to find out granular detail of my interaction with the company if he wished.

Finally, the culture asset was clear in my interaction. In particular in the absolute commitment to the core values of JCB and how that manifested itself in exceptional customer service and the personal relationships with suppliers. In terms of this culture what really impressed me was not that they wanted to resolve the matter in a *customer is always right* kind of way, but that they wanted to address my rather naive criticism head-on and demonstrate what they really believed in as a company and as a brand.

Buy JCB.

The Alchemist's view

In conversation with Roger Philby

What does brand mean to Chemistry?

"OK, so we have an ambition and a plan. That is to get to £40m in value. On the way we have done our business planning and our head count planning, our capacity planning, our functionality planning. We've analysed the demand in the market, as opposed to us having some bloody aspiration that we're going to double the business every year from now until eternity. We've developed fantastic products against that demand and got bloody good systems in place.

"But in order to get to my ambitious plan we've got to be really sharp about our position in the market. Our brand. So, we 'create opportunities for people to be brilliant at work.' That's the intent. But what's the brand about? Now we say 'We drive top line growth through behaviour change.' Now that is something someone can buy. And then we explain how."

Your architecture and your content?

"Yes and based on unique IP and we can talk about what we've done and for who and why we are brilliant and why you need to spend your money with us.

"So we are putting in place a bunch of strategies and plans around how we grow this business in a sustainable way. And I'm really excited about that. And now we are going to market with this brand and our new products and new channel. So there are now two budgets; a training budget and a recruitment budget that we could attack. Forget the general consulting budget and all the other budgets that we could potentially have a go at, these are two we could attack. Of those clients in the London M4 corridor that fit our profile, what are the size of those budgets? It's trillions. It's bonkers."

Action plan: Things to do now

1. **Think about your brand in asset terms**. Is everything the customer hearing based on your core IP?

2. **Think about your brand architecture and marketability.** Make sure your communication is not based purely on the *content* of your product.

3. **Consider whether your brand is enough of an asset to attract others**. Ask "What if someone paid to use our brand? Who would they be? What would they look like? What would they get?"

Chapter 11.
The Summit

"Our goal is not to build a platform; it's to be across all of them."

Mark Zuckerberg

Choosing scale for your business

V+7	Scale
V+6	Brand architecture
V+5	Channel extension
V+4	Product extension
V+3	Systems / product innovation
V+2	Talent / capability / culture
V1	———————————— Industry benchmark

I F A LEVERAGEABLE BRAND IS UNUSUAL IN A PRIVATE BUSINESS THEN scale is even rarer. At every layer of the valuation model it is *your choice* as to how far you want to go. This is as much a vision tool as anything else. How far do you really want to go? There are many fantastic, *scaled* private businesses in the UK and around the world, like JCB and AKQA. But is that *your* vision for *your* business?

What I did not confess to when I mentioned earlier about my climb up Aconcagua was that I didn't actually reach the top. Despite months of planning and weeks of pain I turned back a few hundred metres from the top. I reckoned that a further two hours of clinging to an ice-bound precipice in a screaming white-out nightmare of hurricane force winds and driven ice crystals where I could neither see nor breathe was probably not worth the investment. I chose to stop.

In the same way, it's a rational strategic choice to take your business journey only to the point on the valuation model that works for you. Each layer can be a destination as well as a staging post. It doesn't mean you sell your business (although you could), or tread water once you arrive. It means the activity and growth continues based on the assets you have achieved up to that point. A V+5 or even a V+2 business can be a fabulous, highly wealth-generative enterprise giving dozens or hundreds of people a future whilst giving you the fulfilment of seeing realised what you set out to achieve.

To create real scale in a business is a fabulous achievement but it requires huge dedication over years. That dedication must be rooted in your personal intent. When I spoke to Ajaz Ahmed (who really has built a private business to exceptional scale), it was clear that he was driven by a simple intent to give people quality and fulfilling jobs and opportunities. That is the kind of intent that drives scale.

I think you need to reflect on the impact on your family and your broader life whilst building the business. Is it worth it? Being a scale business owner can be the best thing in the world; just ask Richard Branson. But it's a choice.

When I turned back on that mountain there was another climber who was fixatedly determined to carry on. He was exhausted, delirious, spent. Had he gone on it would have killed him. Yet it took all the efforts of me and the guide to get him to turn back. Sometimes we get so fixated on the goal we forget the cost on our lives and families.

It is worth spending some personal time, perhaps with a coach or mentor, getting really clear on this. Take yourself to the point in time when you are running your scale business and *live* the experience. What is it like there? Look back and describe the journey. Has it been fun and fulfilling or were there too many sacrifices made?

The Alchemist's view

In conversation with Russell Stinson

Russell, it's an amazing story. So what's the vision now then? What's the scale vision? How big do you want to get?

"The vision we've set for ourselves is 500 clients, 5000 people."

What happens then?

"For us this is about building something that we're proud of, our intent is to make a difference in people's lives.

"London is the global capital of the five-star hospitality sector and, as London's dominance continues, we will be well positioned to drive our growth. We know five-star hospitality. We aim to have deep and meaningful partnerships with our clients that enable them to deliver that exceptional five-star service to their customers.

"We're focused on creating something that is built properly, that is built for the long term. Sure, financial freedom is attractive and over the next three to five years we would look to take investment in to achieve that. We're ensuring that we've got a set of options available to us. However, we're committed to making sure this business achieves its full potential and sets new standards in our sector. We really want to make a difference. But we're also clear that as the business grows our focus must be in the black, developing our strategy and providing strategic oversight and guidance to the business and not in day-to-day operational delivery."

So your focus is on ensuring you are personally fulfilled and happy and not a particular scale target. But how would it feel to have 5000 happy, developing employees?

"Immensely proud that actually the thing we set out to do we have done. We sat in my house seven years ago and agreed three core things: to make sure we look after our team; to provide a great service to the client; and to build a great company. The second and third are, to me, natural outcomes of the first so our people has always been the focus.

"We have a genuine passion for our clients and for our people. Many people in our team have travelled a long way to build a better life for themselves and for their families and we take our responsibility to them very seriously. That's what makes us different from our competitors. We're a values-based business and we're committed to doing the right thing.

"We've got an amazing team, remarkable opportunities ahead of us and the most amazing clients anywhere in the world. We are a company who do things properly and we want to build a great business in any sector.

" 'Making a difference' is our purpose and this has helped us articulate right from the start what we've tried to do. I feel immensely proud that we've done what we felt wasn't being done in the industry. It's been an amazing journey and we've only scratched the surface of what we're capable of delivering."

In conversation with Roger Philby

Roger, it looks like, from what you've said, that you have a plan to get you to a £40m valuation business.

"Mmmm. That's not really true. We don't have a plan for forty. What we do is build layer on layer, look at the demand and then go from there."

Do you have a feeling for the end game in valuation terms? Do you have a destination in mind?

"I don't care. It's not the point! We just fell out with a VC on that basis because they wanted to know my exit plan. I said we'll exit when the world's changed. When you walk into a FTSE 100 company and the first thing the board do is go 'Let's talk about our people and our culture, guys.' And actually they spend a day on that and they spend 15 minutes on the P&L. On that day, we'll know we are through."

Action plan: Things to do now

1. **Keep checking in with yourself if this is what you really want.** Is it what your family wants? Take yourself in your imagination to scale and ask what it is like and what the journey involved.

2. If it's not what you want, **work out what you really want and structure a plan to get that.**

3. **Start with revisiting your core intent.** Is that driving your decisions and your life plan?

4. If your intent and your scale business are aligned... **enjoy it.**

Chapter 12.
A Conversation About Exit

"If you realise there is no finishing line, it's liberating to just make it the best it can be."

Ajaz Ahmed

"The people who say 'All I want to do is sell my business and be a millionaire' are a bit like blokes who say 'All I want to do is go out and get laid tonight.' They normally go home on their own."

Keith Abel

CONGRATULATIONS ON REACHING THE END OF THIS JOURNEY AND thank you for bearing with me. We are at the top of the mountain.

What happens next?

The obvious answer is exit and a whole industry has grown up that will help you to do this, particularly in the UK and the US. There is also much great literature and advice on this subject. But allow me to take a contrary view. Why sell?

I simply mean that it is well worth taking a lot of time to look at what your real motivations are. What is your intention? How will that be served by an exit? More time to do other stuff and financial freedom are likely to be on the list, but does that have to mean a sale?

At Shirlaws we once surveyed our clients all over the world and, on starting to work with us, over 30% said they wanted to sell in the next five years. Yet in the end few do, because the work that Shirlaws does – teaching business leaders about the process I have described in this book – enables them to see their business in a different light.

Frank Bastow is an example of this. As he explained earlier, it's great to just fall in love with your business again once you see it from an asset and not an earning perspective. That gives you choice of how to leverage that asset to achieve what you want. If it is freedom of time and money that you desire then that is easy to achieve.

On this journey I have met some amazing people. In the context of exit I would divide them into three groups: those who have sold and are ecstatically happy; those who sold and perhaps regret it; and those who will be carried out of their business feet first, not because they are fixated or a workaholic, but because owning the asset enhances and supports the life they want to lead.

Four Alchemists' views on exit

Nick Jenkins

Nick, what was the experience like of selling the business?

"Ten years in I looked at our growth trajectory and it was still going up but I felt it wasn't going to go through the exciting times that I'd had. I'd been doing it for 12 years, I suppose. It felt like the chance to do something different, personally. And the other thing, also, is when you've got 90% of your assets tied up in one business, it's a precarious position to be in. And it had got to the point where I recognised that I could sell it and be in a position of complete freedom. Forever. And that turned out to be the case."

Tell me about the experience.

"It's a lot of work. A lot of it is actually getting your business in shape. A lot of it."

At what point did you start telling people that this was on the cards? Sorry for the pun.

"Well, we had 100 people in the UK and Guernsey. I was able to tell them very late on. I told the MD and the Finance Director about only two months before. I had been planning it for a long time. I had taken myself out operationally as early as 2007 and become Chairman and hired a CEO. From then on I was doing two and half days a week."

You'd already stepped out operationally. You'd systemised it, got it all organised, independent. What were you doing then?

"Skiing. I had other businesses as well. I had investments in other businesses. And… I actually was just taking it easy."

Emotionally you were half out, really?

"Yeah, yeah, yeah. Being Chairman is a much better position to be in as a founder because I didn't want to be an employee any more so I just took a fee for being Chairman and said I'd put the time in as and when I need to. So my job was strategy and exit. And that's all I did. The day-to-day running of the business was Ian's and that was that."

How long did the sale process take from seriously starting negotiations to deal?

"A year."

If you were in the business, running the business as a CEO, it is not to be taken lightly.

"I don't think it's a very wise idea. No, it's quite time consuming and distracting. It's a lot easier to take on the role of Chairman. Executive Chairman. I actually think the role of Executive Chairman is the best role for the founder because you're still in control of the business in terms of strategy but the business can run without you, which is important, on a day-to-day basis. It gives you time away from the business to think about things strategically. It gives you room to think.

"The other thing is that when you come up with a really good idea you're not thinking 'God, I've actually got to do that!' I was a bit tired after 11 years and the business was throwing up enormous dividends so I... I was making £3m a year from it. So, it was enough. It wasn't as if I was fighting for every penny."

And how did it feel when the deal was done?

"Pretty good. I mean, working up to it for a pretty long time, it's a bit like finishing your A-levels!"

No regrets?

"No. No, absolutely not. I'm still a bit involved. I'm very fond of the team and I still sit on the board of the Moonpig Foundation which is the charity that we set up. I go on the annual bike ride with them around Europe and I pop into the office every once in a while. But by that point I'd built a life outside of it."

Briefly tell me about that life.

"Well, I got to the point where I wasn't that excited about making more money. I wasn't really spending the money I'd got anyway. I think you definitely get less materialistic when you've got it because the excitement's going.

"For some time before I sold the business I started doing more of the philanthropy side. I'm generally quite curious about social issues and I spent a year running a charity as a CEO which actually was fascinating, very informative, complete pain in the arse. I now sort of act as a trustee of that charity, and I do various other things so from this chat I am going to speak at a conference on impact measurement in the development sector and of course I ski a lot and am learning to fly, so there's a whole load of other things that I do now, so I'm manically busy.

"However, there's always that question of identity – I didn't want to be known as someone who used to do something. The challenge is you have to redevelop your identity – it's easy to be defined by what you do. If I never have a business that's as successful as Moonpig again, it won't be important. But what I'm doing for the non-profit sector is very interesting, keeps my mind ticking over. It's a lot more complicated than business."

Rupert Lee-Browne

Rupert, you have this amazing business chock-full of assets. Why not grab the chance for an exit?

"Let's reverse up slightly. When we talk about vision, what is the general view of a fast-growing business started by an entrepreneur? Most people want to know about the fairytale ending. When does the owner sell out? When does he make loads of cash? I think this is the wrong question to be asking. Entrepreneurs are surrounded by people who encourage them to sell their businesses – as an entrepreneur you're told the only real reason you're doing this is to make money.

"Added to which, at some point you're not going to be good enough to run a large business anyway so best to sell out before you get caught out. And funnily enough it's the people who are telling us this that have a vested interest in the *value moment*. It's our lawyers, it's our accountants, it's our private equity people, it's our VCs, it's our bankers, it's our friends, it's our family, it's everybody around us apart from ourselves... And we are brainwashed into thinking this is what we should be doing because this is what entrepreneurs do.

"I believe that entrepreneurs build businesses for every reason other than cash itself. It's not about the cash. It's about proving something to somebody. Okay, so maybe the cash is a demonstrator, it's a measurable way of saying, 'There, I did it, I proved you wrong.' It's why we are entrepreneurs. Ask any entrepreneur, if they knew now what they knew then, would they have started the business? And usually it's like 'Oh, hell no.' But then on reflection they say 'Actually, yes I would!' We need to be encouraging and supporting entrepreneurs to build long-term businesses, not just ones to make a quick buck or two. This benefits them, their employees, their customers and the economy.

"And then the exit question. If I get to X what then happens? The reality is that I sell the whole caboodle and get out, in which case, what the hell am I going to do with my time? All I've got is a pile of cash and the worry of what to do with a pile of cash sitting in the bank. I know a few people to whom this has happened and it's frightening.

"A good friend is this very, very nice American guy who was an engineer. He was part of a team that built a business in server hardware that then got bought out by a really big player. And he found himself with sixty million in cash. And no job. I wouldn't say he was miserable but he was wary of everybody. I mean, everybody. And he put most of his money with a private bank who promptly lost a proportion of it in *investments*. I mean, the amount of money that these guys lost was shocking.

"So having sold out, you're in a position where, who do you trust? Do you trust somebody enough to give your money to look after? Or do you look after it yourself? But if you're in the business of selling server hardware you are probably not going to have the skills required to be an investment manager. In his case, he was putting money into small football clubs. Why? 'Because they asked me,' he explained."

Keith Abel

Keith, you are famous as the guy who sold your business twice. Can you tell me about what, we are told, entrepreneurs are all supposed to aspire to, which is selling the business?

"Well, my big advice to them would be give up now if that's what you aspire to! As an aim it's totally meaningless and you probably won't get there. I really would honestly say that. And the people who say 'All I want to do is sell my business and be a millionaire' are a bit like blokes who say 'All I want to do is go out and get laid tonight.' They normally go home on their own. If that's all you're in it for, it won't happen.

"You've got to do your business because there's something that you can do so much better than anyone else and you've got to absolutely love that it's better than anyone else's. Be that running an airline and making it have more comfortable first class seats, or making furniture and knowing it is the most comfortable furniture in the world or the cheapest furniture in the world or whatever it is. Whatever that is, it has got to be what you want to focus on. And if you focus on that, and you can inspire everyone around you to focus on that, then off the back of that your business will be successful.

"And if your business is successful, I would challenge every single one of those people to think what it means to sell it, because most people will sell it at, or aspire to sell it at, say, a multiple of ten times EBITDA. So let's do the maths. You've got a million pound turnover business that's growing, alright? Because if you want to get ten times it's got to be growing, it's got to be growing well. And it's making £100,000 a year, okay? You sell that business for ten times earnings you're going to get a million quid for it, okay? How much money are you reasonably going to be able to get out of your investment of a million pounds? The answer is 3%, okay? So you're now making £30,000 a year out of your investment having sold your business, okay? Now, it was making £100,000 a year, before tax granted, but you would definitely have been able to draw out £50,000. So you've now gone from a position where you could draw out £50k to now you can only draw out £30k and that business is growing and the only person who knows how to make it grow is you.

"And you may think, 'Well, it's never going to carry on growing,' but everyone thinks that and they bloody well do carry on growing and that's what the private equity world knows – that if something starts growing it generally gathers this snowball momentum and carries on growing. So you could in five years' time have a £5m business that's making £500,000 a year but your poxy little million quid is still going to be a million quid because you're not investing for growth, you're investing for some income. And it's only going to be making you £30,000 a year.

"So my big question would be, if the motivation is 'I'm exhausted and I want to have some time off,' brilliant, then employ the right people to take some of the pressure off you! Because, you see, now I've sold the business I miss enormously not having a full-time PA. I didn't have to fill my car up because you park it next to the diesel tank and some very kind chap in logistics would always shove a bit of fuel in it. I could run so many things legitimately through the business. I had fantastic people around me to do any ideas that I had and suddenly they're all gone in a puff of smoke."

You lose that structure, the family.

"You lose your community. And that's far more important than having a quick buck."

And if I'm tired and I'd like some cash?

"I would say borrow some money against the business. If you need to get some security, sell a minority stake in your business but it'll be the biggest mistake you'll ever make in your life. Be patient, hold on to it, keep it growing and get some other people in to take some of the heavy work and you'll probably find, unless you're an incredibly arrogant prick, that people you bring in to do it for you are a darn sight better at doing certain bits of it than you are. Honestly, ten times over – you look at Nick Wheeler, or the Jack Wills guys and they've all hung on to their business.

"Fine, people brag about me because I've sold my business twice but, you know, if I was running it I'd probably be having an easier time. I'm now finding things that I'm going to do with the proceeds that'll get me employed again but it's going to be bloody hard work. So, that would be my advice."

Ajaz Ahmed

Ajaz, what is the long term?

"I don't understand the word 'exit'. Why would I leave this business? It's about duty. You have a duty to the work, a duty to the staff, a duty to clients and stakeholders. I don't understand the whole *build the business to sell it* thing. I could have quit work when I was 23 and had a good life and if I was super smart, I probably would have done that! But I love the work we do, our team, our clients. It keeps me motivated. There's always something new."

I don't hear a lot of regret in that statement...

"I love it here more than I have ever loved it. How can you love a business more now, when it's the size it is, than when we were a start-up? Because we are realising the ambition and the vision we had when we founded it but still have that start-up mentality. If you realise there is no finishing line, it's liberating to just make it the best it can be."

And the exit?

"When I have nothing left to give. When I'm six feet under."

Conclusions

The making of an Alchemist

IN THE COURSE OF WRITING THIS BOOK, IT'S AMAZING HOW MANY people have asked me "What are they like?" and "What makes a really successful entrepreneur?" By now you will know my answer is that what is common to them all is a real understanding of their assets and a laser focus on building and leveraging these. A more useful response might be to unpick this by way of a conclusion to the book.

The most obvious reaction to meeting any of these people is that you really wouldn't know they are as successful as they have been. You wouldn't be able to tell apart the £10m or £500m business owner. They are universally modest, charming and generous, the source of which is that money has never been the driver. They simply don't much care about it but, more importantly, it's an *outcome* of what they do care passionately about.

It's also very clear to me that, whatever words they may use, they have an instinctive understanding of context and only choose to engage with content when they need to. They see the big picture; they get the *why*. Whilst they are adept at diving into granular detail of cost control or how a cauliflower is cut, they only do so against a clear context. They are in and out of content. It's not where they live.

The bad news for the indolent is that they also work exceptionally hard. In fact they work all the time. If that disturbs you then you are unlikely to be an Alchemist; you are not in the right mindset. The point is that they see don't see a distinction between *work* and *home*. Their business and their home lives are intertwined. Their business provides them with challenge, joy and fulfilment. They have almost the same passion for the business family as their own family.

They see a world of opportunity and not risk. Fun and not fear. It also means that they have no sense of guilt, they feel no need to justify if they choose to go sailing on a Wednesday afternoon or disappear off to Mongolia for three weeks at the drop of a hat because they fancy experiencing the yak festival. They have balance on their own terms. Since they have systemised and self-responsible businesses they don't need to be there to operate them.

In Stages terms this means they are all well beyond the Second Brick Wall and into advanced growth. They have built the assets that allow them to feel quietly but deeply proud. Although they are working hard, they feel they have all the time in the world.

What of the assets that they have built (it goes without saying that the platform is completely robust)?

Most importantly, my strongest sense is that they understand why they do what they do and are passionate about taking others along on that journey. They are driven by personal freedom and committed to giving opportunities to others. In my terms, they are crystal clear of their intent and they love building a community of people around that. They have learnt how to build extraordinary performance cultures which free up their own time to be creative and operate far ahead of the business. They have the self-confidence to employ talent wherever they see it (and love people brighter than themselves) and they have the moral courage to measure and enforce capabilities. Their businesses can be the best places in the world to work – but only if you fit.

They are perpetual innovators and have a hawkish attention to detail when that is required. They love to systemise and then to move on. They are obsessed, not so much by the product, but by how the customer experiences it. They are consumers of their own product and talk regularly to customers. They move fast and innovate constantly, never satisfied with what has worked in the past, and often have to learn how to work within a broader management structure so as not to be too disruptive!

The combination of their time freedom and intellectual freedom means that they have the opportunity and aptitude to create and pursue radical ideas. Extension is natural to them. They have enquiring dispositions and wide interests and take inspiration from a wide range of sources.

It also makes them natural connectors. Relationships are important, collaboration is natural. They will meet another entrepreneur on an aeroplane and a new business opportunity will develop from the conversation. Most of them are constantly aware of and seeking new channel opportunities.

How far they want to take their businesses really depends on their intent. Some of these Alchemists are driven to change the world, some to change the lives of a few, some to create freedom for themselves and their families. Some are building great brands and driving to global scale. Most have reached a point of satisfaction that doesn't require these things. The driver is their intent. And that also drives their decisions around exit.

Action plan

If the preceding pages do not yet describe the life you lead but sound like the life you want then you are on a journey. A journey to find your own alchemy. How far you choose to travel is up to you. Based on what I have seen in hundreds of great businesses, the following action points should be your guide.

Stage 1: Getting to benchmark

1. Take a look at your Stages journey. Draw the model. Where is your business today? Where are you personally? And where are your key team? What is coming up?

2. Ensure you hold a strategic retreat offsite, ideally once per quarter. Include an exploration of Stages with your key team in your next retreat.

3. Decide specifically what you need to do to effectively navigate through the next stage.

4. If one of your businesses is in *start-up*, make sure you fully understand the sector, drivers and the KPIs against which you'll measure success. Check-in with yourself that tenacity is not becoming stubbornness.

5. If you feel the business is ready to shift into sustained growth, work out what investment will create that shift. What is your one big thing? What do you need to invest in commercially and energetically? What must you detach from and attach to, even if it's just in your head?

6. If your business is in sustained growth, invest early in the five key skills.

7. Make sure you have an absolute focus on what makes you famous; obsess about making it the best it can be from a customer's

perspective; listen to your people; talk to your customers and become a customer if you can.

8. Check in on your channel strategy. Make sure it's right for the business at this point in your business lifecycle and for the economy.

9. Invest time and focus in your *functional* system and platform.

10. Ensure you have full capability in your management team. Train generously. Don't be sentimental if it's time for someone to move on.

11. Have a complete review of your platform and make sure you are getting the fundamentals right. Monitoring and measurement is critical so that you can move on.

12. Review your diary for this month. Systematically colour-code each meeting, appointment or task in red, blue or black. What percentage of your time do you spend in each colour? Begin a functionality project – create an organisational structure and workflow in red, blue and black for the business that spreads responsibility better and frees you and your senior team from *the current job* to create time for you to innovate up that asset ladder.

13. Hold a strategic retreat devoted to the platform. Examine all the elements *below benchmark* with your senior team and work out how you can better systemise and monitor these and who will be responsible for each.

14. Start to develop a capacity plan which you can use as a daily management tool and a key monthly measurement of performance.

15. Examine your position and product. Are you absolutely clear of your position in the market? Can you articulate exactly what you are best in the world at and is everyone in the organisation, everything they do and everything you say consistent with this? Is your product absolutely the best it can be?

16. Make a commitment to truly understand your customers' experience. Use your product, website, etc. Talk to your customers directly. Ask your people how they think you can improve.

17. Put together a servicing strategy for your customers. Think creatively about how you can delight them between sales. Involve them in the business as much as possible.

18. Focus on your management team. Continue to upskill yourself and your team. Ask them what further learning they would value. Consider having some education together as a team. Review your functionality and capacity plans to identify any developing skills gaps. Look at least two years ahead; do you have the team to get you to where you want to be? Hire early.

19. Look outside of your business. Make the time to read widely. Attend business talks and thought-leading events. Don't get stuck in today.

20. Get it valued. Seriously consider having your business formally valued and invest in a report that shows you specifically what you need to do to drive your asset strategy. At Shirlaws we used Assay Advisory (**www.assaycf.com**) and it changed how we ran the business.

Stage 2: Building the asset business

Culture, talent and capability assets

1. Develop a real focus on your culture, particularly if you have taken the eye off this particular ball in the last few difficult years. Think of inspiring but implementable ways to create a transformational culture and allocate a generous budget. Appoint a Head of Amazing?

2. Ensure your culture is based on the three principles of *purpose, autonomy* and *mastery*. Are you setting the context? Do you have the courage and confidence to genuinely give your people autonomy? Is yours really a learning culture in which your people grow and develop every day? If not, now is the time to do something about it. A culture is not expensive to create. It just takes time and commitment.

3. Have culture as the topic of your next retreat. Take your key team offsite to uncover and agree the *intent* in your business. What purpose do you serve? Are you inspiring and rallying your people and their passions around that purpose? Ensure it is something that you and your team can take pride in. Try to find some emotive language that will engage your people at a deeper level. External facilitation is a great idea.

4. Unless you have recently conducted a full and proper values exercise that you are proud of, do one this quarter. Appoint a champion to run it for you but you MUST be actively involved as sponsor. Have your champion run a workshop or series of workshops so that everyone has the chance to contribute. Ensure you define what your values mean and attribute measurable behaviours.

5. Choose to focus on your leadership style. Leadership is about confidence, vision and inspiration. The source of all of this is an understanding of your own intent and purpose. Find it! In other words, make sure you are very clear of your context. Manage the energy of your team every day. Collaborate but have the confidence to trust your instincts and ensure you are decisive and clear. Consider coaching if you feel it will help you.

6. Improve your communication abilities. What is the *Nelson Touch* to you? Consider adopting 10 Things in 100 Days or another

way to improve communication in your business. Communicate regularly and honestly with your team. Consider a daily or at least a weekly blog. If your people are at multiple sites use technology. I have found PresentMe (**www.presentme.com**) to be a great tool for creating engaging communication of factual information.

7. Take a good look at your talent. Define very clearly *what good looks like*. Work out how to measure that. Agree the values and motivations that are important in the talent you seek to hire.

8. Think about what learning, skill transfer and coaching means in your organisation. Create a strategy for continual development of the whole team. Remember that the most motivated people are those that feel they are challenged and constantly developing *mastery*.

9. Start to definitively measure the capability of your organisation. Create a capability scorecard of some sort so that you can measure capability at an individual and organisational level. Measure progress *relative to self*. Use this measure to plot progress which will generate energy and confidence for yourself and the team.

10. Start to systemise your culture, talent and capability as much as possible. At every opportunity put in place documented systems and written policies for culture, recruitment, talent management, capability, etc. Pass this skill on to the next level of management so that you can move on, leaving a replicable system in place.

Innovation assets in product and systems

1. If your organisation is not naturally innovative then, once your commercial and cultural platform is in place, it's important to invest some real focus in this. A 100 days of Innovation project driven by

you but involving everyone might be a good way to kick off.

2. Make a bold declaration of intent. Think big. Make it fun.

3. Involve your customers and suppliers. Ensure innovation is focused widely. Gather and use lots of data.

4. Divide the task up *functionally* and have people volunteer to join innovation teams. Make sure these are well led and encourage those who agree to lead. Give plenty of autonomy but show your passionate involvement. Acknowledge people for their commitment and for their ideas. Remember innovations can be iterative and radical, cultural and commercial.

5. Whatever else you seek to innovate, it's critical to make your business *system* a key focus and ask if it is the best it can be. Be as creative as you can be, get out of the existing pattern, use analysis and ask customers and suppliers.

6. Ask yourself if any of your current systems are, or could be, an asset in their own right. Get creative; sure you designed them in a P&L context but could they be or become an asset? How could you derive revenue or other value from them?

7. Innovate your product iteratively. Generate lots of ideas to ensure the customers' experience of the product is the best it can be. Never rest.

8. Innovate your product radically. Get really creative based on a fundamental understanding of your IP (assets). If that requires you to get really clear about the assets and drivers of your business that is a good topic for a retreat. Based on those assets what might people give you money for? What completely new product innovations could you create? Are there products hidden in your systems?

9. Ensure your innovations programme includes your customer service strategy. As part of the *platform* you devoted some focus to servicing customers between sales. How can you now innovate that service to constantly improve and impress? What creative and fun ideas can you generate?

10. Get out of the pattern. Don't be a Wenham Lake Ice Company. Find ways of stretching your perspective: educate yourself, read widely, meet interesting people, make the time.

Extension assets: product

1. It's a good time to revisit the layers below where your business is now. To extract real value from a layer you *must have fully implemented* strategies in all the layers underneath.

2. To continue the asset journey, ask yourself the question of whether you would increase equity more quickly through a logical next step extension or by understanding your fundamental assets and extending from those. A good question to ask is "What if we were an xyz company? Then what would we do?"

3. The extension strategies that create the most exponential value growth are sourced in an understanding of the core IP. A great topic for a quarterly retreat is to get a real understanding of your IP and be able to articulate it in a few words. Part of this is understanding what you can be *best in the world* at.

4. Use that understanding of your IP to drive and strategically manage your product extension strategy. List all of your core asset drivers, all the elements of your IP, and ask yourself what a company with those assets would do. What products would it make and sell? Use that insight to drive an extension strategy conversation.

5. Make sure you can see beyond your product. Use all the innovation techniques to get the perspective you need to really see what sits behind your current product and proposition.

6. Think about what and who you *know* more than what you do.

7. You may be well served by getting some external perspective. It's often incredibly hard to identify the true IP in your business and not get tied up in your product. It's often easier to see it from the outside.

Extension assets: channel

1. This might be a good opportunity for the leadership team to pause and reflect; an opportunity to re-articulate your collective and personal visions and to check how far you want to go both culturally and commercially. Very specifically, do you want a multi-channel business and if so, what does that look like?

2. Think creatively and innovatively about which channels are appropriate and available for each of your products and businesses. If you have innovated and extended a product, the next question is what channels can you create or innovate for it?

3. Do the analysis. Not all channels are equal. Work out which channel will give you the most return for a given commercial and energetic investment. Prioritise accordingly.

4. Consider whether your channel is an asset for you because it allows you to extend into new or higher-margin markets for your products or whether a channel could be an asset for someone else. That could be an acquirer or commercial partner. Think of yourself as a channel for someone else and ask "What if?" questions.

5. Revisit your IP and use that understanding to drive and strategically manage your channel extension strategy. List all of your core asset drivers, all the elements of your IP, and ask yourself what a company with those assets would do. What channels would it sell into? Use that insight to drive a channel extension strategy conversation.

6. Don't ignore unpaid referrals as a source of pre-qualified leads. Identify who can act as your channel, share what you believe in and overcome fears.

7. Get digital. If you are a foreigner in a digital world, find a native to guide you. That can be an external adviser, or a new hire. At Shirlaws we have loved bringing in interns; we give them a step into employment and they act as our guides in the digital world. Get innovative about the opportunities for you online.

8. Look at your assets and IP creatively and see what you have that others want. Think about what partnerships will open new markets for you. Think broadly and creatively.

9. How can you package your assets in such a way that someone else will pay handsomely for them? What within your layers of assets (culture, talent, systems, product) could be valuable to someone else? How might you structure a licence deal?

10. Take time to consider the implications of going international. Do you have the culture, capabilities, systems and products in place to open up international markets? If not, what do you need to innovate? Have any recent systems or product innovations opened up new opportunities overseas? Do you have the knowledge and trusted contacts in your chosen market? If not seek advice.

Brand assets

1. Think about your brand in asset terms. Is everything the customer hearing based on your core IP?

2. Think about your brand architecture and marketability. Make sure your communication is not based purely on the content of your product.

3. Consider whether your brand is enough of an asset to attract others. Ask "What if someone paid to use our brand? Who would they be? What would they look like? What would they get?"

Scale

1. Keep checking in with yourself if this is what you really want. Is it what your family wants? Take yourself in your imagination to *scale* and ask what it is like and what the journey involved.

2. If it's not what you want, work out what you really want and structure a plan to get that.

3. Start with revisiting your core intent. Is that driving your decisions and your life plan?

4. If your intent and your scale business are aligned... enjoy it.

Where to go for help

The more I see of businesses and the more experienced I have become in running my own, the more of a believer in getting qualified outside support I have become. All the great businesses I know accept help and challenge from outside. It is unrealistic to expect anyone running a business to be right all the time; we need the knowledge of experts. It is easy to get stuck into your own *pattern*; we need the challenge and perspective of skilled outsiders.

Where to go for this help is a real question. It can look expensive. It can have uncertain outcomes. I tend to work with people who I like and feel a sense of engagement with. I base my decisions more on shared values than the experience they can show.

This is not in any sense a comprehensive list but here are the contact details of three organisations mentioned above.

Smith & Williamson

Smith & Williamson are largely a UK firm but form part of a wider international network. I think of them as *accountants plus*, but they describe themselves as "a leading independent financial services firm combining an accountancy practice, investment management arm and a private bank." What I like are their values and the fact that they really get entrepreneurship.

I'd ask to speak to Guy Rigby in London (020 7131 4000) but a full list of their offices is on the website: www.smith.williamson.co.uk/offices

Cranfield School of Management

There are many business schools and management colleges offering education for business owners. Cranfield (in the UK) has always impressed me with its approach and the energy and connection of the alumni network. Its courses, particularly for entrepreneurs the Business Growth Programme (BGP), are really worth a look.

www.som.cranfield.ac.uk

Shirlaws

Shirlaws is a global organisation that works with CEOs and management teams to build successful, asset based business. "Our seasoned entrepreneurs and world-class methodology help you build a business that is easy to run and a joy to own," is what they say.

www.shirlawscoaching.co.uk in the UK

www.shirlawscoaching.com anywhere else in the world.

At Shirlaws, one of the things we do as part of our cultural asset layer is to have a company library from which we encourage staff and clients to borrow books. It's an idea I pinched from Tony Hsieh of Zappos. We love it when people make notes in these for others to gain from. Our library seems to grow all the time as friends and colleagues make suggestions and, even better, gifts.

In case it should be of any help, I include the current list of books in the library below. I have underlined the ones I mentioned in the text.

Adelsberg, David van and Trolley, Edward A., *Running Training like a Business* (Berrett-Koehler, 1999)

<u>Ahmed, Ajaz and Olander, Stefan, *Velocity* (Vermilion, 2012)</u>

Allen, David, *Getting Things Done* (Piatkus, 2002)

Blanchard, Kenneth and Johnson, Spencer, *The One Minute Manager* (Harper, 2011)

Buckingham, Marcus and Clifton, Donald O., *Now, Discover Your Strengths* (Pocket Books, 2005)

Buckingham, Marcus, *The One Thing You Need to Know* (Pocket Books, 2006)

Cameron, Julia, *The Artist's Way* (Pan, 1995)

Carnegie, Dale, *How to Win Friends and Influence People* (Vermilion, 2006)

Christensen, Clayton, *The Innovator's Dilemma* (Harper Paperbacks, 2003)

Coelho, Paul, *The Alchemist* (HarperCollins, 2012)

Collins, Jim, *Good to Great* (Random House Business, 2001)

Covey, Stephen R., *The 7 Habits of Highly Effective People* (Simon & Schuster, 2004)

Darwin, Charles, *The Origin of Species*

Denvir, Paul, *Growing your Client Base* (The PACE Partners, 2007)

DePorter, Bobbi and Hernacki, Mike, *Quantum Learning* (Piatkus Books, 1998)

Dennis, Felix, *How to Get Rich* (Ebury Press, 2007)

Edwards, Gill, *Conscious Medicine* (Piatkus, 2010)

Fynn, *Mister God, This is Anna* (HarperCollins, 2005)

Gerber, Michael E., *The E-Myth* (HarperBusiness, 2011)

Gibran, Kahil, *The Prophet* (Pan, 1991)

Gladwell, Malcolm, *The Tipping Point* (Abacus, 2002)

Godin, Seth, *Purple Cow* (Penguin, 2005)

Godin, Seth, *Poke the Box* (The Domino Project, 2011)

Godin, Seth, *We Are All Weird* (The Domino Project, 2011)

Hendricks, Gay, *The Big Leap* (HarperOne, 2010)

Hicks, Esther and Hicks, Jerry, *The Astonishing Power of Emotions* (Hay House UK, 2008)

Hill, Napoleon, *Think and Grow Rich* (Vermilion, 2004)

Hill, Napoleon, *Outwitting the Devil* (Sterling, 2013)

Hill, Vernon, *Fans Not Customers* (Profile Books, 2012)

Hsieh, Tony, *Delivering Happiness* (Business Plus, 2010)

Kahneman, Daniel, *Thinking, Fast and Slow* (Penguin, 2012)

Kiyosaki, Robert, *Rich Dad, Poor Dad* (Plata Publishing, 2011)

Kline, Nancy, *More Time to Think* (Fisher King, 2009)

Kyle, MacKenzie, *Making it Happen* (John Wiley & Sons, 1998)

Lama, Dalai, *The Leader's Way* (Nicholas Brealey Publishing, 2009)

Lencioni, Patrick, *The Five Dysfunctions of a Team: A Leadership Fable* (Jossey Bass, 2002)

Livingston, Gordon, *Too Soon Old, Too Late Smart* (Hodder Paperbacks, 2006)

Livingston, Gordon, *How to Love* (Da Capo Press, 2009)

Logan, Dave, King, John and Fischer-Wright, Halee, *Tribal Leadership* (HarperBusiness, 2011)

Machiavelli, Nicolo, *The Prince*

Marcum, Dave, Smith, Steve and Khalsa, Mahan, *Business Think* (Franklin Covey on Brilliance Audio, 2012)

Marx, Karl, *Das Kapital*

Moore, Geoffrey, *Crossing the Chasm* (Capstone, 1998)

Moore, Geoffrey, *Inside the Tornado* (HarperBusiness, 2011)

Mullins, Laurie J., *Management and Organisational Behaviour* (FT Publishing International, 2013)

Nordstrom, Kjell and Ridderstrale, Jonas, *Funky Business* (Financial Times / Prentice Hall, 2007)

Ogilvy, David, *An Autobiography* (John Wiley & Sons, 1997)

Peck, M. Scott, *The Road Less Travelled* (Rider, 2008)

Pink, Daniel, *Drive* (Canongate Books, 2011)

Rigby, Guy, *From Vision to Exit* (Harriman House, 2011)

Ruiz, Don Miguel, *The Four Agreements* (Amber-Allen Publishing, 1997)

Semler, Ricardo, *Maverick!* (Random House Business, 2001)

Sharma, Robin, *Leadership Wisdom From The Monk Who Sold His Ferrari* (Harper Element, 2010)

Sinek, Simon, *Start with Why* (Penguin, 2011)

Templar, Richard, *I Don't Want Any More Cheese: I Just Want out of the Trap* (Prentice Hall, 2003)

Tolle, Eckhart, *The Power of Now* (Hodder Paperbacks, 2001)

Trout, Jack and Ries, Al, *Positioning: The Battle for Your Mind* (McGraw-Hill Professional, 2001)

Walsch, Neale Donald, *Conversations with God* (Hodder and Stoughton, 1997)

Williamson, Marianna, *A Return to Love* (Thorsons, 1996)

Worthington, Ian and Britton, Chris, *The Business Environment* (Financial Times/Prentice Hall, 2009)